THE ILLUSTRATED DICTIONARY OF

ANIMAL
LIFE

Reader's notes

The entries in this dictionary have several features to help you broaden your understanding of the word you are looking up.

- Each entry is introduced by its headword. All the headwords in the dictionary are arranged in alphabetical order.

- Each headword is followed by a part of speech to show whether the word is used as a noun, adjective, verb or prefix.

- Each entry begins with a sentence that uses the headword as its subject.

- Words that are bold in an entry are cross references. You can look them up in the dictionary to find out more information about the topic.

- Many of the entries are supported by illustrations. The labels on the illustrations highlight the key points of information and will help you to understand some of the science behind the entries.

- Many of the labels on the illustrations have their own entries in the dictionary and can therefore be used as cross references.

THE ILLUSTRATED DICTIONARY OF

ANIMAL
LIFE

Contributors
Martin Walters
Lesley Ann Daniels
Merilyn Holme
Clara Sansom

CLAREMONT
BOOKS

Copyright © 1995 Godfrey Cave Associates
First published 1995 in this format by
Claremont Books
42 Bloomsbury Street
London WC1B 3QJ

Design: Steven Hulbert
Illustrations: Peter Bull Art Studio; Jeremy Gower (B.L. Kearley Ltd);
Lynda Arnold, Stephen Lings, Alan Male, John Rignall (Linden Artists Ltd);
Miranda Gray (Maggie Mundy Illustrators' Agency)

Consultant: Malcolm Whitehead BSc, Director of Education,
Twycross Zoo (East Midlands Zoological Society), Atherstone, UK

Printed in Great Britain.

ISBN 1 85471 644 1

A

aardvark *noun*
An aardvark is a sturdy **mammal** with a long snout and large ears. It lives in the **rain forests** and **grasslands** of Africa. Its home is a deep, underground **burrow**. Aardvarks are **carnivores**, feeding on ants and termites. The aardvark tears open an ant's nest with its **claws**, pushes its snout and licks up the ants with its long, sticky tongue.

abdomen *noun*
The abdomen is a part of an animal's body that contains most of the internal organs. **Digestion** takes place in the abdomen. The abdomen of an **insect** is one of the three main parts of its body. The other two are the **head** and the **thorax**.

adaptation *noun*
Adaptation describes a physical or behavioural change which takes place in an animal. This change is normally permanent. It will help the animal to survive better in a particular **environment**. An adaptation can also be a temporary change. This might be when an animal **migrates** to a place with a better climate. Living things which cannot adapt may become **extinct**.
adapt *verb*

addax *noun*
An addax is a **mammal** which lives only in the Sahara, a desert area of northern Africa. Addax are **antelopes**. They are **herbivores** and eat coarse plants. Addax can survive without drinking water. The small amount of water that they need comes from dew and from the plants they eat.

aerial *adjective*
Aerial describes anything that lives or moves about in the air. A bird is an aerial animal. The environment of the air can also be described as aerial. Animals which are not aerial either live on the land and are **terrestrial**, or live in water and are **aquatic**.

aggression ► page 7

albatross *noun*
Albatrosses are large **birds**. There are 13 different species of albatross. They are found in all the **ocean** regions of the world. Albatrosses have very long **wings**. The longest measure more than three metres from wing tip to wing tip. Albatrosses spend most of their life far from land. They glide for hours, looking for **prey**. They catch fish or squid from the surface of the sea. Albatrosses come to land to mate and lay their eggs. They gather in large colonies.

albino *adjective*
Albino describes an animal which does not contain any **colour** or **pigment**. An albino animal is often white. Many white animals are not true albinos because they have coloured eyes, bills or legs. The eyes of true albinos look pink because blood vessels are showing. Very few albino animals are found in the wild. They are easy to see, so they are caught and eaten by **predators**.

alligator   *noun*
Alligators are **reptiles**. They also make up a
family and there are two species. One lives
in the United States of America, the other
lives in China. Both species are found in
freshwater habitats and **swamps**. Alligators
have a long tail, huge jaws and short,
stumpy legs. Their skin is covered in horny
plates. Alligators are **carnivores** and catch
fish, birds and even large mammals. When
they float, they often keep their snout above
the water for breathing.

ammonite   *noun*
Ammonites were a kind of **mollusc** which
first appeared in the seas about 245 million
years ago. They died out, or became
extinct, about 65 million years ago. They
were **invertebrates** and had hard, chalky,
spiral shells. Today, we can sometimes find
ammonites as **fossils** in rocks which once
lay under the sea.

amoeba   *noun*
An amoeba is a tiny **organism** made up of
only one cell. An amoeba belongs to a group
of living things called **protista**. It lives in
water or on damp ground. An amoeba
moves by flowing into a new position. It eats
by wrapping its body around a piece of food
and digesting it. An amoeba **reproduces** by
splitting in two. It is so small that it can only
be seen with a strong microscope.

amphibian   ► page 8

anaconda   *noun*
Anacondas are large **snakes**. Their skin is
olive-green or yellow and is marked with
black spots or diamonds. There are two
species of anaconda, both of which live in
South America. They are some of the largest
snakes in the world and can grow up to nine
metres long. Anacondas are **carnivores**.
They wrap themselves around their bird or
mammal prey, and squeeze it to death.

anglerfish   *noun*
Anglerfish are sea **fish** which have a large
head and wide mouth filled with rows of
sharp teeth. There are about 215 species of
anglerfish which live in the warmer parts of
every **ocean**. Most anglerfish have a flap of
skin attached to a long spine on top of their
head. The flap looks like a piece of food
and it is bioluminescent. This acts like a bait and
the anglerfish snaps up any fish which try to
eat this 'food'.

animal   *noun*
Animals make up one of the five **kingdoms**
of living things. Animals are **organisms**
which can move around and can respond to
the world around them. Animals eat plants or
other animals. Scientists have discovered
over one million different **species** of animal
on our planet but there may be many more.
Animals are classified into **vertebrates** and
invertebrates. There are five main **classes**
of vertebrates – **mammals**, **birds**, **reptiles**,
amphibians and **fish**. There are many
classes of invertebrates.

ant   ► page 12

antbird   *noun*
Antbirds are small, dull-coloured **birds**.
There are 230 different species of antbird.
They live in the **forests** of Central America
and South America. Many species eat ants,
and the rest feed mainly on other insects or
small fruits. Some species of antbird are
known for following swarms of army ants
through the forest.

aggression *noun*

Aggression is **behaviour** which is threatening or frightening to other animals. An animal may show aggression in the **defence** of itself, its family or its territory. The animal can make itself look scary, by having a fierce expression or by becoming a bright colour. Fighting is another kind of aggression. An animal may use its teeth, claws, horns or sting when it fights.

aggressive *adjective*

Fighting behaviour

Male red deer lock their antlers in a fierce fight. The winner of all these fights will be the leader of the herd.

Threatening behaviour

A male baboon threatens a rival male by baring his powerful canine teeth in a huge yawn.

A stag beetle grips his enemy with his huge, pincer-like horns. Then he picks up the weaker beetle and hurls him to the ground.

A female ostrich defends her nest by ruffling her feathers. This makes her seem even larger and more dangerous.

Male rattlesnakes wrestle in a fight for a female. They do not bite each other with their sharp, poisonous teeth called fangs. These are only used to kill prey for food.

amphibian *noun*

An amphibian is a **vertebrate** whose skin is smooth and moist. Amphibians belong to a **class** of animal and there are about 3,000 species. They include **frogs**, **toads**, **salamanders** and **caecilians**. These all live in fresh water. An amphibian is born in water and spends the early part of its life there. When it becomes an adult, it lives mostly on land. But it still lays its eggs in water. An amphibian's body changes as it becomes an adult. This process is called metamorphosis.

This frog is laying its eggs in the water. Each egg is surrounded by protective jelly.

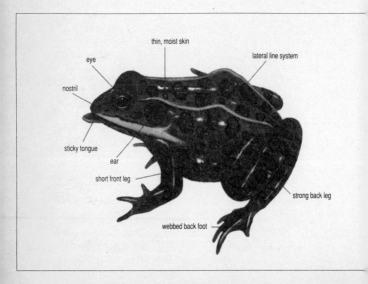

thin, moist skin

lateral line system

eye

nostril

sticky tongue

ear

short front leg

strong back leg

webbed back foot

These larvae have only just hatched out of their eggs. They are called tadpoles. They live like fish, breathing through gills and using their tails to swim. The tadpoles eat plants.

These tadpoles are gradually turning into adults. The back legs are the first part of the body to grow. The tadpoles still live and breathe underwater, but they can now eat small animals.

These tiny frogs have all their legs. They will slowly absorb the tail into their body until they look like small adults. Now they can sit on rocks above the water and breathe air with their lungs.

This adult frog is leaping up to catch a fly. Only three months ago, it was a tadpole. The adult frog lives on land. But it must still live near water or in a damp place, as it breathes partly through its skin. It will return to the water to mate and lay its eggs.

anteater *noun*
Anteaters are **mammals**. There are four
species of anteater, the largest of which is
the giant anteater. Anteaters live in the **rain
forests** and **grasslands** of Central America
and South America. They have a long, tube-
shaped snout and a long tongue. Anteaters
are **carnivores**, but they have no teeth. An
anteater breaks into an ant or termite nest
with its sharp claws, then licks up the insects
on its long, sticky tongue.

antelope *noun*
Antelopes are **mammals**. Like goats and
deer, antelopes are members of the **bovid**
family. Most species of antelope live on the
plains of Africa but a few are found in Asia.
Antelopes are sleek and graceful and have
slender horns and hoofed feet. **Addax**,
impala and **kudu** are examples of antelope.
The largest is the Derby eland, which stands
about two metres high at the shoulder. They
are **herbivores** and feed on grass and
plants. Antelopes are **ruminants**, so they
eat their food twice.

antenna (plural **antennae**) *noun*
Antennae are the pair of thin and delicate
stalks on the head of almost every **insect**.
They are **sense** organs. Some insects use
their antennae to smell or hear. A male
mosquito can use its antennae to hear a
female almost half a kilometre away.
Antennae can also pick up information on
heat, vibrations, chemicals and gases.

anterior *noun*
The anterior is the front part of an animal.
An animal's head, mouth and many of its
sense organs are usually found in the
anterior area of its body.

anus *noun*
The anus is the opening in an animal's body,
usually at its back end, where waste is
passed out. This waste is the food left over
after the rest has been **digested**. In most
mammals, only solid waste passes through
the anus. Birds, reptiles and insects pass out
liquid waste as well.

ape *noun*
Apes are large, tailless **mammals**. They are
primates that have long arms, and long
fingers and toes. Apes live in groups in the
rain forests of Africa and Asia. **Gorillas,
chimpanzees, orang-utans** and **gibbons**
are all species of ape. Apes are some of the
most intelligent animals. Most apes build
nests either in the trees or on the ground to
sleep in. They are mainly **herbivores** and
eat fruit and plants. But gibbons and orang-
utans sometimes eat insects and small
birds.

aphid noun
Aphids are tiny **insects**. They have a soft, plump body, small head and tube-shaped mouth. Aphids pierce the stem and leaves of plants with their mouth and suck out the juices. This can kill the plant. Aphids produce a liquid called honeydew. Some ants feed on honeydew and can be found 'milking' the aphids for this sticky liquid. The ants often look after aphids by moving them from one plant to another so they have a good supply of honeydew.

aquatic adjective
Aquatic describes anything which lives or moves about in water. The environment of water can also be called aquatic. Animals which are not aquatic either live on land and are **terrestrial** or live in air and are **aerial**. Some animals, such as **amphibians**, spend part of their lives as aquatic animals and part as terrestrial animals. **Dolphins**, **fish**, and **lobsters** are aquatic animals.

arachnid noun
Arachnids are animals that make up a group, or **class**, of **invertebrates**. This class includes **spiders**, **scorpions**, **mites** and **ticks**. Arachnids live in all parts of the world and in every kind of **habitat**. Their body is divided into two parts and they have eight legs. Unlike insects, arachnids do not have **antennae** or **wings**. They have a hard covering on their body which they **moult** as they grow. Most arachnids are **carnivores** and eat insects or small invertebrates.

archeopteryx noun
Archeopteryx was an animal that lived about 140 million years ago. It is now **extinct**. Archeopteryx was similar to a **reptile**. It had a **skeleton** like a small **dinosaur**, teeth and a long tail with a row of feathers on each side. The archeopteryx also had **feathers** and **wings**. Many scientists classify it as a **bird** and believe that it could fly. Some scientists think archeopteryx shows that birds **evolved** from reptiles.

archerfish noun
Archerfish are small **fish**. There are six species of archerfish. They live in parts of Asia and Australia. Archerfish catch insects sitting on leaves. The fish swims to just below the insect. Then it spits water straight up at the insect which falls into the water.

armadillo noun
Armadillos are **mammals**. There are 20 species of armadillo, found in the **forests** and **grasslands** of South America. Armadillos are covered with a shell made of hard, bony plates. When they are scared, some armadillos curl themselves into a ball. They are protected by their hard shell. Armadillos are **nocturnal**, and live in **burrows**. They are **carnivores** and feed on termites and insects. They lick up insects with their long, thin tongue.

arrow-poison frog noun
Arrow-poison frogs are small **amphibians**. They belong to the **frog** family and are found in forests in South America and Central America. Their skin gives off a **poisonous** substance which is harmful to birds and small mammals. Many arrow-poison frogs are bright colours.

arthropod noun
Arthropods are animals that make up a part of the group, or **phylum**, of **invertebrates**. The arthropod phylum is the largest in the animal kingdom. Arthropods include **insects**, **crustaceans** and **arachnids**. Arthropods live on land and in water in all parts of the world. All arthropods have jointed legs and bodies made of different segments. Most arthropods have only three or four pairs of legs attached to their **thorax**. All arthropods have a hard covering over their body which they **moult** as they grow.

ant   *noun*

Ants are small, dark-coloured **insects** with a hard covering. There are about 10,000 species of ant. They are found in all parts of the world and in every kind of **habitat**. Ants are **social insects** and live in **colonies**. An ant colony contains a queen, workers and soldiers. They can live in underground tunnels or inside a huge mound of soil. Ants are strong and can each carry something that weighs as much as 10 to 50 ants.

Slavemaker ants steal ant larvae from other nests and bring them up as workers.

Harvester ants collect seeds and store them inside the nest.

Honey ants also collect honeydew. They store it in part of their body.

Army ants do not build a nest but travel around. They eat anything in their path.

Leafcutter ants carry leaves back to the nest. These leaves fertilize gardens where the ants grow fungus.

Dairy ants live on a sweet, sticky liquid called honeydew produced by aphids.

asexual reproduction *noun*
Asexual reproduction is reproduction which only involves one parent. The opposite of asexual reproduction is **sexual reproduction**. Some **organisms**, such as **amoebas**, can reproduce by splitting in two parts. Other organisms, such as **sponges**, start as a little growth on the parent sponge. In both these ways, each part grows into an independent adult.

ass *noun*
Asses are **mammals**. They belong to the **horse** family. There are two species of ass. One is found in Africa, the other lives in Asia. They live in large herds in **deserts** and open **plains**. Asses have hoofed feet, a large head and long, narrow ears. Asses are **herbivores** and feed on grasses.

auk *noun*
Auks are **birds**. There are 22 species of auk, one of which is the **puffin**. All auks have short wings and a short tail. They are found in the North Pacific, North Atlantic and Arctic oceans. They mostly live at sea but return to land to nest in **colonies**. Auks feed on fish and plankton. They dive into the water and chase the fish under water.

avocet *noun*
Avocets are **birds**. They are found in **marshes** and **estuaries** in most parts of the world, except the Arctic. Avocets are **waders**, with long legs and a long bill which curves upwards. They eat insects, small **aquatic** animals and some aquatic plants.

axolotl *noun*
An axolotl is an **amphibian** which is found in lakes in Mexico. It has small legs and feet and a long tail. It has a dorsal **fin** that runs from its head to its tail, and under the tail to its back legs. The axolotl breathes through **gills** on the outside of its body. The axolotl is born as a **larva**. It grows but it never changes into an adult. While it is a larva, it becomes **fertile** and can **reproduce**.

aye-aye *noun*
An aye-aye is a small, brown **mammal**. The aye-aye builds its nest in the trees of the **rain forests** of Madagascar. It is an **omnivore**, feeding on insects and fruit. It uses its long fingers to find and dig out insects which live in the trees. The aye-aye is **nocturnal**. Today, the aye-aye is very **rare**, and is protected in nature reserves.

13

B

babbler *noun*
Babblers are **birds.** There are about 250 species of babbler. Most species are found in the **forests** of Africa, southern Asia and Australia but one lives in North America. Babblers have short, rounded wings and strong legs and feet. They cannot fly very well so they spend most of their time on the ground. Babblers eat insects, berries and fruit, which they find by poking the ground.

baboon *noun*
Baboons are large **mammals** that belong to the **monkey** family. They are found in the **savanna** and rocky areas of Africa and south-western Arabia. Baboons have a large head and long, sharp teeth. Their arms are about the same length as their legs. They live in groups, mostly on the ground but also move about in trees. Baboons are **omnivores** and feed on insects, birds' eggs and fruits.

bacteria *noun*
Bacteria are tiny **organisms** that only have one cell. They are so small that they can only be seen through a microscope. There are thousands of species of bacteria. They live almost everywhere and are even found inside animals. Some bacteria are harmful to the animals they live in. Bacteria reproduce by **asexual reproduction**.

badger *noun*
Badgers are **mammals**. There are eight species of badger. They live in a variety of **habitats** in all parts of the world except South America and Australia. Badgers have a stout body, a short, bushy tail, and usually, white and black markings on their face. They are **nocturnal** and live in **burrows**. Badgers are **carnivores** that eat rodents and insects.

bandicoot *noun*
Bandicoots are small **mammals**, found in the **forests** of Australia and New Guinea. Bandicoots are **marsupials** and have a long, narrow head and sharp teeth. They dig **burrows** with their claws or build nests on the ground. Bandicoots are **omnivores** and eat insects, spiders, worms and plants.

barb *noun*
A barb is a hook which is found on the end or along the edge of an object. A **bee's** sting is straight with a row of barbs on it. After a bee has stung an animal, these barbs hook the sting in the flesh. Barbs are also the thin threads attached to the shaft of **feathers**.

barnacle *noun*
Barnacles are **crustaceans** that live in all the **oceans**. They are found attached to underwater objects, such as rocks. They even fasten onto living things, such as **whales**. Adult barnacles have a hard shell which covers the body. The shell has a lid that can be closed for protection. Barnacles feed on tiny **organisms** which they catch by waving their feathery legs.

barracuda *noun*
Barracudas are large **fish**. There are about 18 species of barracuda. They live in warm parts of the Atlantic, Indian and Pacific **oceans**. Barracudas have a long, thin body and a pointed head. Their lower jaw juts out and is full of large, sharp **teeth**. They are fierce fish, preying on other fish for food.

bat *noun*
Bats are **mammals**. There are more than 900 species of bat. They live in all parts of the world, except in the polar regions. Bats are the only true flying mammals. They have a flap of skin between their fingers and back legs on each side. These **wings** help the bat to fly. Bats usually live and **hibernate** in dark, sheltered places, such as caves or buildings. They are **nocturnal**. Most bats are **insectivores**. Some bats do not have a good sense of smell or sight and find their food by **echo-location**.

beak ► **bill**

bear *noun*
Bears are large, stocky **mammals**. There are seven species of bear, most of which have long, thick fur. The largest is the Alaskan brown bear which can grow to a height of almost three metres. Bears are found in Asia, Europe, North America, South America and the Arctic. They live in **dens**, usually alone. Bears are **carnivores** and most also eat grass, fruit, leaves and nuts.

beardfish *noun*
Beardfish are **fish**. They are found in **tropical** and sub-tropical areas of the Atlantic, Pacific and Indian oceans. They usually live in deep water, and some can be found at a depth of 600 metres. Beardfish have large eyes and have two barbels under the chin.

beaver *noun*
Beavers are furry **mammals**. There are two species of beaver. One species is found in North America, the other species lives in Asia and Europe. Beavers are **rodents**. They have webbed feet and a flat tail. They use their tail to steer when they swim. Beavers live in rivers, streams and lakes near woodland. They are **builders** of dams. They build with wood from trees which they cut down with their large front teeth. Beavers feed on the bark, twigs and roots of the same trees.

bee *noun*
Bees are small, 'hairy' **insects** that fly. There are about 20,000 species of bee, found almost everywhere in the world. They make honey from a sweet liquid called nectar which they collect from flowers. Most bees live alone, but some species are **social insects** and live in **colonies**. All female bees have a sting which they use for self-defence. There are four stages in the **metamorphosis** of a bee. These are the egg, larva, pupa and adult.

bee-eater *noun*
Bee-eaters are colourful **birds**. There are about 25 species of bee-eater. They are found in Europe, Asia, Africa and Australia. Most live on **plains**, open brushland or woodland. Bee-eaters have a long, slightly curved bill, in which they catch **bees** and other flying **insects**. They live in large groups called **colonies**. Bee-eaters nest in **burrows** which they dig in river banks or flat ground. The female bee-eater lays her eggs at the end of the burrow.

bill *noun*

A bill is the hard part of a **bird**'s mouth. Some other animals, such as **turtles**, also have a bill. Birds catch food in their bill, and also use it to build **nests** and in defence. The shape and size of a bird's bill depends on what it eats and how it feeds. Bills are also called beaks.

The hummingbird has a long, thin bill. As it hovers, the bird delicately probes its bill deep into the flower and sucks out a sweet, sticky liquid called nectar.

The bald eagle has a bill similar to many other birds of prey. It is strong, short and hooked. The bill is used to tear the flesh off captured prey.

The avocet has a long, upturned bill. It sweeps its bill from side to side under water or in soft mud, feeling for small water animals.

The toucan has a huge, brightly coloured bill. Although it looks so bulky, the toucan's bill is light and strong. It uses its bill for plucking berries from trees and stealing eggs and young from other birds' nests. The size and colour of the toucan's bill may scare the parents, who do not attack.

The pelican has a long bill with a saggy pouch below it. It uses this pouch to scoop fish out of the water. The fish are then swallowed whole.

beetle *noun*
Beetles are **insects**. There are about 300,000 species of beetle. They are found in all parts of the world and in all habitats except the **oceans**. Beetles have a special pair of hard front wings, called elytra. These protect the beetle's body. Most beetles live alone but a few species are **social insects**. Beetles are **omnivores** and feed on plants and animals.

behaviour *noun*
Behaviour is the way that animals act. It includes the way they feed, how they defend themselves and their way of life. One example of animal behaviour is the **migration** of birds, such as swallows, to warmer climates to search for food.

bill ► page 16

binocular vision ► eye

bio- *prefix*
Bio- is a prefix used to describe living things.

biological control *noun*
Biological control is a way of controlling **pests** using living things. Some **organisms** are used either to destroy or reduce the number of pests. For example, ladybirds feed on aphids. Farmers may encourage ladybirds to live on their crops to stop the aphids from destroying the plants.

biologist *noun*
A biologist is someone who studies **biology**.

biology *noun*
Biology is the study of living things. In biology, scientists study the structure of plants and animals, and their way of life. They look at all forms of life, from tiny **bacteria** to huge blue **whales**. There are two main branches of biology. **Zoology** is the study of animals, and botany deals with plants.
biological *adjective*

bioluminescence *noun*
Bioluminescence is light which is given off by some animals and plants. It is caused by a chemical reaction. The majority of animals which give off light live in the sea. Over 1,000 species of fish give off bioluminescence. Some animals, such as **squid**, use bioluminescence to frighten off their enemies. Others, such as **anglerfish**, use bioluminescence to attract prey. On land, fireflies and glow-worms also give off light.
bioluminescent *adjective*

biomass *noun*
Biomass is the term used to refer to the amount of living things in a certain area. It is the total weight of the **organisms**. Biomass also refers to substances produced by animals or plants that can be used as a source of energy. Manure from animals, and plant material such as cornstalks are examples of biomass energy sources.

biosphere *noun*
The biosphere is the name given to the area in which all living things exist. The Earth's surface and the atmosphere around the Earth form the main part of the biosphere. All animals and plants live in the biosphere.

biped *noun*
A biped is an animal with two feet. **Birds** and humans are bipeds.

bird *noun*

A bird is a two-legged **vertebrate** which is covered in **feathers**. Birds are a **class** of animal. Scientists have named about 8,600 **species** of bird. All birds have **wings**, though some birds cannot fly. Birds are **warm-blooded**, so they stay the same temperature no matter how cold or warm it is. This means they can live in all **habitats**, from hot deserts to the cold polar regions. Different species of bird have particular ways of finding and catching their food. They may have a **bill**, wings and feet of different shapes.

Most birds, such as the blue tit, mate once a year. Some birds attract a female with a courtship display. Birds produce young by sexual reproduction.

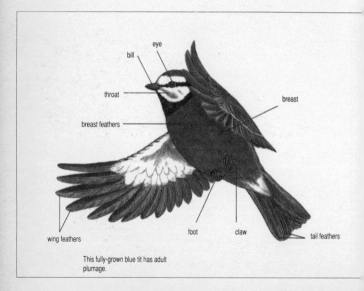

This fully-grown blue tit has adult plumage.

Many birds, including the blue tit, build their nest in the branches of a tree, where there are few predators. All birds lay eggs with hard shells. Some birds lay up to 15 eggs. The parents incubate the eggs, keeping them warm.

When the embryo is fully grown inside the egg, the baby bird hatches. It punches its way through the hard shell. It uses a spike on its bill called the egg tooth.

The baby bird, called a fledgling, does not look like the adult bird. It is not yet fully developed and cannot fly. The fledgling's enormous, gaping mouth encourages the parent to feed it.

When the fledgling has grown, it flies from the nest. Birds know by instinct how to fly, but they must practise before they can fly well.

bird ► page 18

bird of paradise   *noun*
Birds of paradise are **birds**. There are
42 species, found in the **rain forests** of
northern Australia, New Guinea and on
islands nearby. Most males have colourful
plumage, and showy head and tail feathers.
They use their plumage in **courtship** to
attract the females. Birds of paradise feed
on fruits, berries, insects and frogs.

bird of prey   *noun*
Birds of prey are birds that hunt and kill
other animals for food. They have hooked
bills and **talons**. They eat the flesh of birds,
reptiles and small mammals. Some birds of
prey also feed on **carrion**. **Owls**, **eagles**,
vultures and **condors** are all birds of prey.

birdsong   *noun*
Birdsong is the variety of sounds and notes
that birds make. Different species of bird
make different patterns of notes. Birds sing
to **communicate** with one another. In most
species, only the male sings. Males sing one
song to attract a mate and another to defend
the area they live in. Some young birds have
to listen to the adult males to learn songs,
but others know the songs by **instinct**.

birth   *noun*
Birth is the production of live young. In
mammals, birth is the moment when the
baby animal comes out of the mother's body.

bison   *noun*
Bison are large **mammals**. There are two
species and they are members of the **bovid**
family. They live in herds in the open **forests**
of northern Europe and in the **prairies** of
North America. Bison have humped
shoulders and a large head and they look
like an ox. Bison are **herbivores**. The
American bison is wrongly called a **buffalo**.

bivalve   *noun*
Bivalves are **molluscs** that have a shell
made up of two parts. There are about
11,000 species of bivalve, including **clams**,
oysters and **mussels**. Bivalves usually
keep their shells open. But if disturbed, they
pull the shells shut using **muscles**. Bivalves
are found in water almost everywhere.

blood   *noun*
Blood is a liquid that flows around an
animal's body. In most animals, blood
carries food and a gas called oxygen to
cells in the body. The blood flows inside
tubes called blood vessels. Many
invertebrates such as **insects** do not have
blood vessels because their blood fills the
whole body. An insect's blood is green,
yellow or colourless because it does not
carry oxygen. Some animals, such as
sponges, do not need blood to survive.

blubber   *noun*
Blubber is the layer of fat which **dolphins**,
whales, **seals** and other sea mammals have
to keep them warm. It lies under the **skin**
and over the **muscles**. Some whales have a
layer of blubber 50 centimetres thick.

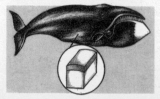

boa constrictor *noun*
Boa constrictors are large **snakes**. They grow more than three metres long. Boa constrictors are found in **deserts** and **rain forests** in South America. They live mainly on the ground, but can climb trees. Boa constrictors eat birds, small rodents and other mammals. They wrap their body round the prey and squeeze it to death. Boa constrictors can live for many months without eating. Unlike most snakes, they do not lay **eggs** but give birth to live young.

body temperature *noun*
Body temperature is the heat of an animal's body. An animal gets its heat by burning food or from the sun. Some animals, such as **birds** and **mammals**, are **warm-blooded** and their body temperature is almost always the same. In **cold-blooded** animals, such as **reptiles**, their body temperature changes with the temperature of the air around them.

bone *noun*
Bone is a hard substance found inside the body of some animals. Bones make up the **skeleton** of **vertebrates**. The place where two bones meet is called a **joint**.

bony fish *noun*
Bony fish are **fish** with a skeleton made of **bone**. There are about 20,000 species of bony fish. They include anglerfish, eels and bowfin. They are found in all **oceans** and also in **fresh water**. All bony fish have a spine and pairs of **fins**. Their tail fins are usually the same size as each other. Unlike **cartilaginous fish**, bony fish have a **swim bladder** which helps them stay afloat.

booby *noun*
Boobies are large **birds**. There are six species of booby. They have webbed feet, a long, sharp bill and long, pointed wings and tail. Boobies live near warm seas in large groups called **colonies**. Some species nest on the ground and some nest in trees. Boobies plunge into the sea from high in the air to catch their food. They eat mainly flying fish and squid.

bovid *noun*
Bovids are a family of hoofed **mammals**. There are about 120 species of bovid. These include **antelope**, **bison**, **goat** and **oryx**. They are found in a variety of habitats, such as **grasslands**, **forests** and **mountains**. They are **ruminants** and have four parts to their stomach. Most bovids have horns.

bowerbird *noun*
Bowerbirds are stout **birds**. There are 18 species of bowerbird, found in New Guinea and Australia. Bowerbirds have strong legs and feet because they spend most of their time on the ground. Male bowerbirds build grass and twig structures called bowers, which they decorate with colourful objects, such as fruits and berries. The males perform courtship dances in the bower to attract the female. They are **omnivores** and feed on fruits and insects.

builder *noun*

A builder is an animal that builds something.
An animal may build a shelter to protect it
from **predators** and from hot, cold or wet
weather. Some animals, such as **beavers**,
build a shelter for themselves and their
family. **Termites** build a structure for the
whole **colony**. Or an animal may build a
structure which helps it catch its prey. For
example, the **spider** makes a **web**. Spiders
make their own silk to build with. Most animal
builders use natural materials like twigs,
leaves and mud that they find around them.

Termites chew, burrow and build to make enormous homes
of earth. These contain cooled rooms and passages.

The male weaver bird makes his nest with long strips of
leaves or blades of grass. He weaves these in and out of
the structure as he builds it.

This spider has built a trap to catch its prey. When an insect comes near the hole, the spider pulls it in and lowers the lid of the trap. The insect cannot escape.

Most spiders build webs to trap prey. Some webs have threads covered with small, sticky droplets. Other webs catch insects in a mass of tiny barbs and loops.

Beavers are skilful builders. These beavers have blocked a stream with sticks, boulders and earth. This makes a deep pool of water. Here, the beavers build a home, called a lodge. This is a domed shelter of sticks, branches and mud. The entrance is under the water, so only the beavers can get inside.

This bottle-shaped nest is built by a female potter wasp. She wets small pieces of mud and makes strips of clay. She lays one coil on top of another. Then she pushes an insect larva inside and lays her eggs inside the larva.

bowfin *noun*
The bowfin is a large, **bony fish**. It lives in quiet streams and ponds in north-eastern America. The bowfin has a rounded tail, a long dorsal **fin** on its back and two bony plates under its throat. It can use its **swim bladder** as a **lung** to take in oxygen from the air. The male bowfin builds a nest on the river bed and cares for the eggs and the young when they hatch.

breathing *verb*
Breathing is the way animals take oxygen into their **blood**. Land animals breathe oxygen through their **lungs**. Fish breathe through their **gills**. **Insects** take in oxygen through tiny holes on the side of their body.

brittlestar *noun*
Brittlestars are **invertebrates**. They are found in all **oceans** throughout the world. They live either under rocks or in burrows in the sand. Brittlestars have long, thin arms and a small body. Their mouth is on the underside of the body. They look like **starfish**. Most species have five arms, which are brittle and can easily break off. But new arms soon grow. On the underside of each arm, thin tubes called **tube feet** breathe, feel and search for food. Brittlestars feed on small animals.

budding *noun*
Budding is a form of **asexual reproduction**. **Jellyfish**, and some species of **sponge**, reproduce by developing buds. Buds are small knobs that grow on the parent. Some buds break away from the parent once the buds have developed into young animals. Others remain with the parent.

buffalo *noun*
Buffalo are large, sturdy **mammals**. They look like oxen and, like them, are members of the **bovid** family. Buffalo live in herds in the grasslands and forests of Africa and Asia. They are **herbivores** and feed on grass.

builder ▶ page 22

bug *noun*
Bugs are **insects**. They are found throughout the world. Some species of bug live in water but most live on land. Bugs do not have any teeth. They suck up blood from animals or plant juices using a jointed beak.

bulbul *noun*
Bulbuls are small **birds**. There are about 120 species which live in **forests**, gardens and **jungles** in Africa and southern Asia. Bulbuls have dull-coloured, fluffy feathers. Some have a crest of feathers on their head. Bulbuls eat insects and fruit.

bunting *noun*
Buntings are small **birds**. There are 552 species of bunting. They live in different **habitats** in all parts of the world, except Australia and New Zealand. Some species are brightly coloured, others are grey or brown. They all have a strong, cone-shaped bill which they use to crack open seeds.

burrow *noun*
Burrows are a type of home made by some animals. They are tunnels or holes dug underground. **Rabbits** and **badgers** live in burrows.

burrowing *noun*
Burrowing is a way of moving under the ground by digging into the soil. Burrowing animals, such as **earthworms** and **moles**, usually have poor eyesight and hearing.

bushbaby *noun*
Bushbabies are small **mammals** with a long tail. They are members of the **loris** family. Bushbabies live in **forests** and woodland in Africa, south of the Sahara. They have pads on their hands and feet to help them grasp the branches. Bushbabies have large eyes because they are **nocturnal**. Bushbabies are **omnivores** and they eat insects, reptiles, birds, plants and fruit.

bustard *noun*
Bustards are large **birds**. There are 22 species of bustard. They are found on **grassland**, dry **plains** and **savanna** in all continents except America. Bustards have a strong body, long legs and a short bill. They nest and feed on the ground. They eat insects, plants and occasionally small animals. In spite of their large size, bustards are very timid and scuttle into hiding at the slightest sign of danger.

butterfly *noun*
Butterflies are colourful **insects**. There are between 15,000 and 20,000 species of butterfly, found nearly everywhere in the world. Butterflies have delicate wings that are covered with small, powdery scales. These scales may be different colours and give the wings their patterns. There are four stages in the **metamorphosis** of a butterfly, the egg, larva, pupa and adult. Most adult butterflies only live for one or two weeks but the adults of some species can live up to 18 months.

C

caecilian *noun*
Caecilians are **amphibians**. They are found in **forests** in South America, Asia and Africa. Caecilians do not have legs and they have a series of rings along the length of their bodies. They look like large **earthworms**. They have tiny eyes which are covered with skin. Most caecilians are burrowing animals. They live underground in **burrows** and eat worms and insects.

caiman *noun*
A caiman is a **reptile**. It is a member of the crocodile order. Caimans live on the edges of lakes and **swamps** in South America. They look like small **alligators** and have a long body, short legs and a covering of horny scales. They are amphibious and are good swimmers. Caimans are **carnivores** and feed on fish, birds and other animals. The female lays her eggs in a nest.

camel *noun*
A camel is a large **mammal**. The bactrian camel is the only species of camel that still lives in the wild. It is found in the Gobi Desert. It has long legs, a thick, shaggy coat and two humps on its back. Each hump is a store of fatty food which helps the camel survive for many days without eating. Camels are **ruminants** and feed on trees, small plants, grass and bushes. Another species, the dromedary, is a **domestic** camel and is no longer found in the wild.

camouflage ► page 28

canine ► tooth

capuchin *noun*
Capuchins are **mammals**. There are four species of capuchin and they belong to the **monkey** family. They live in trees in the **forests** of Central and South America. Capuchins have a round head, a white face and a short tail. They are **omnivores**.

capybara *noun*
A capybara is a **mammal**. It lives near lakes and rivers in Central and South America. The capybara has a large head, a square snout and webbed toes. It is the largest living **rodent** and grows over one metre long. The capybara is a **herbivore**. It is a good swimmer and plunges into water to escape **predators**.

caracal *noun*
A caracal is a long-legged **mammal**. It has long tufts of hair on the tips of its ears. It is a member of the **cat** family. The caracal lives in the **savanna**, open **plains** and **deserts** of Africa and Asia. It is a **carnivore** and feeds at night on birds, gazelles and goats.

caribou *noun*
A caribou is a slim, elegant **mammal**. It is a member of the **deer** family. It is found in **tundra** in North America, Europe and Asia. Caribou have a pair of antlers, long legs and hooves on their feet. Unlike other deer, both male and female have antlers. Caribou are **herbivores** and feed mainly on grass and coarse plants. In Europe and Asia caribou are called reindeer.

carnivore *noun*
1. A carnivore is any animal that eats the flesh of other animals.
2. Carnivore is also an **order** belonging to the class of **mammals**. There are 10 families in the carnivore order, including **bears**, **cats**, **seals** and **weasels**. Most of these animals are **predators** and eat only meat, but some also eat plants. Carnivores have strong jaws for holding their prey and sharp **teeth** for tearing flesh.

carp *noun*
Carp are large, strong **fish**. They live in the slow-moving **fresh waters** of Europe, Asia and North America. They can survive in water that is polluted and contains hardly any oxygen. Carp lay **eggs** in shallow water where they attach them to water plants. They feed on insects and plants.

carrion *noun*
Carrion is the decaying flesh of an animal which is dead. Hyenas, jackals, vultures, many insects and **bacteria** feed on carrion. They break down and digest the dead animal. This forms an important part of the **food chain**.

cartilage *noun*
Cartilage is strong, rubbery tissue found in **vertebrates**. It is more flexible than **bone**. All vertebrates are born with **skeletons** made of cartilage. In most animals, this changes to bone as the animal grows. Cartilage is still found at the ends of long bones and between the bones of the spine. It cushions these bones from shock and prevents bones rubbing together.

cartilaginous fish *noun*
Cartilaginous fish are fish with a skeleton made of **cartilage**. There are more than 500 species of cartilaginous fish. They include **sharks**, **rays** and **skates**. The skeleton has the same layout as that of **bony fish**, with a spine and pairs of fins. Cartilaginous fish live in all the oceans.

cassowary *noun*
Cassowaries are large, shy **birds** that cannot fly. The three species of cassowary are found in **rain forests** in Australia, New Guinea and other nearby Pacific islands. A cassowary's head and neck are bald with brightly coloured flaps of skin called wattles. The head is crowned with a hard, bony helmet which the cassowary uses to force its way through thick undergrowth. It eats insects, fruits and small vertebrates.

cat *noun*
Cats are agile **mammals** that have a muscular body, covered with soft fur. Wild species of the cat family include **tigers**, **lions** and **cheetahs**. Cats are found in all parts of the world, except Antarctica, Australasia and some islands. Cats have sharp teeth and long, sharp claws that they can pull back inside their paws. They are **predators** and are often **nocturnal**.

catfish *noun*
Catfish are **fish**. There are about 2,000 species of catfish, found in most parts of the world. Catfish have pairs of whiskers, or barbels, around their mouth which they use to feel for their **prey** in the mud. They do not have scales on their body, but some have bony plates which look like armour. Most catfish live on the bottom of inland waters, but some live in the ocean. One species can breathe and walk on land.

camouflage   *noun*

Camouflage is a kind of disguise which makes an animal hard to see. Some animals, such as the **tiger**, have coats marked with patterns that look like the plants or earth of their **habitat**. An animal such as a **stick insect** looks like twigs or leaves and it is easily mistaken for those objects. Camouflage helps animals survive because they can hide from **predators**. Camouflaged predators can hunt without being seen by their **prey**.

camouflage   *verb*

Many animals that live in Arctic regions change the colour of their coat with the seasons. In the cold season, the Arctic fox has white fur and matches the snowy landscape. When the snows melt in warm weather, its coat turns brown.

This fish looks like a leaf. It lives in streams in the rain forests of South America. It drifts along in the water, unnoticed by its prey.

The patterns on the female bittern's feathers look like reeds. This hides her while she incubates her eggs.

This stick insect is well camouflaged. It is shaped like a thin twig. It is also green, the same colour as the leaves around it. It waits patiently for an insect to come close so that it can catch it and eat it.

A tiger stalks its prey. The stripes on its fur look like the tall, dry grass of the Indian plain and hide the tiger.

This praying mantis in Malaysia changes colour so that it looks like the flowers around it. This attracts its insect prey.

cavy *noun*
Cavies are small, furry **rodents**. There are about 15 species of cavy. The best-known species is the guinea pig. Cavies live in South America in various **habitats**, including **plains**, **marshes** and rocky areas. They are **herbivores** and feed on grass and leaves. Cavies live in **burrows** and are **nocturnal**.

cell *noun*
A cell is a single, tiny part of all living things. Some simple animals, such as **amoebas**, contain only one cell. Most animals are made of millions of cells. All cells are made of exactly the same basic parts. But cells can be many different shapes and can do different jobs.

centipede *noun*
Centipedes are **arthropods**. There are about 2,800 species of centipede, found in all parts of the world. All centipedes have **antennae** and a body divided into many sections. Each section has a pair of legs. On the first pair of legs there are two **claws** which contain **venom**. Centipedes feed on worms, molluscs and insects and usually hunt at night.

chameleon *noun*
Chameleons are **reptiles** that can change the colour of their skin. Most are found in the **forests** of Africa but they also live in Asia and Europe. Chameleons have a flat body, large eyes and a long, sticky tongue. Some chameleons have horns or a crest on their head. Chameleons usually live in trees or bushes. They grip the branches with their feet and tail. Chameleons are **insectivores**. They shoot out their long tongue to capture insects up to a body length away.

chamois *noun*
A chamois is a **mammal**. It is a member of the **bovid** family and it looks like a **goat**. The chamois is found in the mountains and forests of Europe and western Asia. Groups of about 10 to 15 chamois live together. The chamois is a **herbivore** and feeds on grass and flowers when it can find them. If not, the chamois eats the bark of trees.

characin *noun*
Characins make up a **family** of **fish**. There are about 1,500 species of characin, which include **piranhas**, tetras and pacus. Characins are found in rivers in South America and Africa. Some species, such as piranhas, eat meat. Others eat plants and **plankton**.

characteristic *noun*
A characteristic is any feature of an organism. The feature can be a part of the appearance of an animal's body or its **behaviour**. A characteristic can be learned, or it can be passed to the animal from its parents.

cheetah *noun*
A cheetah is a **mammal**. It is a member of the **cat** family. Cheetahs live on the grassy **savanna** of Africa and south-west Asia. They have a slender body and long legs. Their coat is yellow and is covered with black spots. They are **carnivores**, and feed on small gazelles, impalas, wildebeest calves, and hares. They usually hunt by day. Cheetahs are the fastest land animals over short distances and can run at a speed of about 110 kilometres per hour.

chimera *noun*
Chimeras are fish. They make up the
chimera **order**. Chimeras live in **oceans**
throughout the world. They are **cartilaginous
fish**. They have a long body and a thin tail.
Chimeras feed on small fish and molluscs.

chimpanzee *noun*
Chimpanzees are **mammals**. They are
members of the **ape** family. Chimpanzees
are found in the **forests** and **savanna** of
Africa. They have black hair, their arms are
longer than their legs and they have no tail.
Chimpanzees live both on the ground and in
trees. They usually sleep in nests in the
trees. Chimpanzees are **omnivores** and
feed mainly on fruit, leaves, insects and
plants. Sometimes, they kill and eat monkeys.

chinchilla *noun*
Chinchillas are small, furry **mammals**.
These **rodents** are found in the rocky areas
of South America. They live in **colonies**
either in **burrows** or in rock crevices.
Chinchillas are **herbivores** and feed on
seeds, fruit and grasses. When they eat,
they hold their food in their front paws.

chipmunk *noun*
Chipmunks are small, striped **mammals**.
They are members of the **squirrel** family
and live in **burrows** in the forests of North
America and Asia. Chipmunks are
herbivores and eat seeds and nuts which
they carry in pouches in their cheeks.

chitin *noun*
Chitin is a hard, bony substance. The
external **skeletons** of insects, crabs and
lobsters are made of chitin. Chitin cannot
expand so these animals **moult** their shells
as they grow.

chrysalis *noun*
A chrysalis is the **pupa** stage in the
metamorphosis of a butterfly. The shell of
the chrysalis is hard and protects the
butterfly.

cicada *noun*
Cicadas are **insects** that have short
antennae and two pairs of thin wings. There
are about 1,500 species of cicada. Most are
found in **tropical** and subtropical areas.
Male cicadas make a loud noise to attract
females and to call large numbers of males
together. They make the noise by moving
quickly **membranes** on their **abdomen**. A
female cicada makes tiny holes in the twigs
of trees and bushes and lays her eggs in
them. These holes often destroy crops.

ciliate *noun*
Ciliates are animals made of one cell with
hair-like strands which they wave to move
around. There are 7,200 species of ciliate.
They belong to a group of living things called
protista. Ciliates are the only **protozoa** to
have a mouth. They live in moist places and
can even live inside plants or animals.
Ciliates are so small that they can only be
seen through a powerful microscope.

civet *noun*
Civets are furry **mammals**. They make up a
family. Linsangs and **genets** belong to the
civet family. They live in a variety of
habitats, in Africa, southern Asia and
southern Europe. Civets have a long body,
short legs, a pointed nose and a long, fluffy
tail. They have sharp **claws** which they use
to climb trees. A few species live in **burrows**
in the ground. Civets hunt at night for birds,
frogs, rodents and small reptiles.

clam noun

Clams are **molluscs**. They are found on the bottom of **oceans** and in **fresh water** in all parts of the world. They usually lie buried just beneath the surface. Clams have a **shell** made up of two parts, called a **bivalve**. They have a powerful foot which they use to burrow in mud or sand and two tubes called siphons which let in water. The water provides food and oxygen for the clam. The largest clam is the giant clam. It can grow over one metre long.

class noun

A class is part of the system of animal **classification**. Class is the group which is smaller than a **phylum**. For example, all **vertebrates** which feed their young on their milk and have hair on their body are in the class called **mammals**. Species of mammals include tigers, whales, elephants and bats. Each class is made up of smaller groups called **orders**.

classification noun

Classification is the system by which animals are organized into groups. The animals in each group share similar body **characteristics**. The largest group is a **kingdom** and all animals are in the animal kingdom. The next group is called a **phylum**. For example, all animals with backbones are put in the **vertebrate** phylum. The other groups, each smaller than the one before, are **class**, **order**, **family**, **genus** and **species**. There are more than one million species in the animal kingdom.
classify *verb*

claw noun

A claw is the hard nail on the feet of **birds**, **reptiles**, many **mammals** and some **amphibians**. The pointed end on the legs of an **insect** or **crustacean** is also called a claw. **Crabs** and **lobsters** have claws on the first pair of their legs.

cloven hoof ► hoof

cobra noun

Cobras are very poisonous **snakes**. They are found in Africa and Asia. Cobras have special ribs which expand to make a hood around their head. They have poisonous **teeth** or fangs which they use to bite their **prey** or to spit **venom** into their eyes. Cobras feed on fish, birds, frogs and small mammals. The king cobra is the world's largest poisonous snake. It can grow up to five and a half metres long.

cockatoo noun

Cockatoos are large **birds**. They are members of the **parrot** family. There are 18 species of cockatoo, which live in **forests** in Australia, Indonesia and nearby islands. Cockatoos have a crest of **feathers** on their head, a strong, curved **bill** and a thick tongue. Cockatoos eat fruit, nuts and seeds.

cockroach noun

Cockroaches are **insects**. There are more than 3,500 species, found in a variety of habitats throughout the world. Most live outside, but a few species live in buildings and are **pests**. Cockroaches have a flat, oval body and long **antennae**. They are most active at night when they feed on plants and dead insects. Cockroaches have lived on Earth for over 300 million years.

cocoon noun

A cocoon is the coating which protects the **pupa** of many insects during **metamorphosis**. Most cocoons are made of silk. Some larvae also protect themselves with a cocoon. Some spiders weave a cocoon around their eggs.

cod *noun*

Cod are large **fish**. They live in the northern waters of the Atlantic and Pacific oceans. Cod have five **fins** and a long body which varies in colour from grey to red, brown or black. They are marked with spots on their upper body. Cod lay from three to seven million **eggs** in the depths of the ocean. But only a small number of these eggs develop into young fish. Cod are **carnivores**, feeding on small fish and other sea creatures.

coelacanth *noun*

The coelacanth is a large, heavy **fish**. Its colour ranges from dark brown to blue-grey. Scientists have found fossils of coelacanths that lived more than 300 million years ago. The fish was thought to be **extinct**, until a live one was discovered in 1938. Coelacanths live in the western Indian Ocean, feeding on other fish. Unlike most fish, coelacanths give birth to live young.

cold-blooded *adjective*

Cold-blooded describes an animal whose body temperature is the same as its surroundings. Cold-blooded animals have some control over their temperature. They can move into the shade if they are too warm or into the sunlight if they are too cool. Most animals are cold-blooded, except for **birds** and **mammals**. The opposite of cold-blooded is **warm-blooded**.

colony *noun*

A colony is a group of animals of the same species which live together. In some colonies, animals work together for the good of the whole group. **Social insects**, such as **ants** and **bees**, live in colonies where each insect has a particular part to play in the life of the colony.

colour ► page 34

communication *noun*

Communication is when animals pass and receive messages. Animals can communicate by smell, by touch, by sounds or by their appearance, or else by body movements. **Baboons** can communicate **aggressive** feelings by baring their teeth. A **bee** can tell other bees where it has found honey by performing a special dance.
communicate *verb*

compound eye ► eye

condor *noun*

Condors are large **birds of prey**. There are two species of condor. One species is found in the Andes Mountains of South America and the other species lives in California. This species is only found in captivity. Condors are members of the **vulture** family. They are one of the largest birds in the world. The condor found in the Andes has long wings which measure about three metres from wing tip to wing tip. Condors lay their eggs in caves or in holes. They feed on **carrion**.

colour   *noun*

Colour is the way light is reflected from an object. The eye takes in this light and the brain changes it into colours. Many animals can see colours and some, such as bees, can see colours which humans cannot see. Animals use colour in different ways. Many animals are **camouflaged** and are the same colour as their habitat. Some animals are brightly coloured and this can attract a **mate** for **courtship**. Bright colours often warn **predators** that an animal is poisonous or that it tastes nasty. Common warning colours are red, yellow, white and black.

The skin of this arrow poison frog contains a poison. The bright colours of the frog warn predators away.

The octopus can change colour very quickly when it is angry or frightened. It can also vary its colour to match its background or it can become transparent to escape from predators.

The scarlet macaw is one of the most brightly-coloured birds. Its feathers contain pigments which produce the bright colours.

In some animals, the male is much more colourful than the female. This male mandrill has stronger colours on his face than the female. These colours may scare other males, show how important this mandrill is or attract a mate.

The Morpho butterfly seems to be a rich blue. In fact, the wings are not really blue. They only show blue when the light falls on them at a particular angle.

The coral snake is a poisonous snake and brightly coloured. The milk snake mimics these colours even though it is not poisonous. Predators avoid eating the milk snake because they think it is dangerous.

The flamingo is a pink colour. Flamingos are naturally white, but they become pink when they eat particular crustaceans which contain red or yellow pigments.

conservation *noun*
Conservation is the protection and care of living things to prevent them becoming **extinct**. Conservationists try to protect animals from too much hunting. They also try to prevent the animals' **environment** becoming polluted or being destroyed.

coral *noun*
Corals are tiny **invertebrates** which are found in warm, shallow waters of the ocean. They live together in **colonies** which make delicate and colourful patterns. Corals have hard skeletons. When they die, the skeletons form a rock-like structure. The word coral is also used to describe these forms. Corals are in the same **class** as **sea anemones**.

cormorant *noun*
Cormorants are large **birds**. There are about 30 species of cormorant, found on sea coasts and large rivers in all parts of the world. Cormorants have a long neck, short legs and webbed feet. They are usually black. Cormorants feed mainly on fish. They dive down to catch their prey, and then bring their catch back to the surface to eat.

courtship ► page 38

coyote *noun*
Coyotes are **mammals**. They are members of the **dog** family. Coyotes are found in a variety of **habitats**, such as **prairies** and **deserts**, in North America and South America. They have long legs, large ears and a bushy tail. They are fast runners. Coyotes are **omnivores** and feed on rabbits, rodents, insects, fruit and berries. They are **nocturnal** animals.

crab *noun*
Crabs are **crustaceans**. There are 4,500 species of crab. They are found in all **oceans**, in **fresh water** and some live on land. Crabs have five pairs of legs and a hard shell covering their body. The first pair of legs has large **claws**. Crabs walk and run sideways. Most are **carnivores**, but some species eat plants. The Japanese spider crab is the world's largest crustacean. It can measure up to eight metres long between the tips of its outstretched legs.

crane *noun*
Cranes are large, elegant **birds**. There are 15 species of crane in the family. Many are **rare**, especially the whooping crane of North America. Cranes live in shallow water and marshy areas in Africa, Asia, Europe, Australia and North America. They have long legs, neck and bill. Cranes build flat nests of twigs and raise one or two chicks each year. They feed on frogs, snails, insects and plants. Cranes are well known for their complicated **courtship** dances.

crayfish *noun*
Crayfish are **crustaceans**. There are more than 500 species of crayfish. They live in **fresh water** and are found in lakes and rivers in all parts of the world except Africa and Antarctica. Crayfish have a tough **exoskeleton** covering their body, two long **antennae** and five pairs of legs. The front pair of legs has **claws**. Their body is divided into segments. Crayfish are most active at night. They come out of their burrows and from under stones to feed on snails, tadpoles or insect **larvae**.

crocodile *noun*
Crocodiles are large **reptiles**. They are found in swamps, marshes and rivers in **tropical** countries throughout the world. Crocodiles have short legs, a long tail and a long snout. Their body is covered with horny scales. Crocodiles are **carnivores** and feed on fish, birds and mammals. They lay **eggs** in a **nest** built by the female.

crow *noun*
Crows are large, black **birds**. They are members of the crow **family** which also includes ravens, jays and magpies. Crows are found in all parts of the world, except Antarctica, South America and New Zealand. They nest in trees or shrubs and lay from three to six **eggs**. They eat almost anything, including dead animals, or **carrion**. Crows are thought to be some of the most intelligent birds.

crustacean *noun*
Crustaceans are a smaller part of the **arthropod** or **phylum**. There are more than 42,000 species of crustacean, including **crabs**, **prawns** and **barnacles**. Most live in the sea, but some live in fresh water. **Woodlice** live on land. Crustaceans have jointed legs and many have **claws** to catch their prey. They have two pairs of **antennae**. Crustaceans are **carnivores** and eat smaller crustaceans and **plankton**.

cuckoo *noun*
Cuckoos are slender **birds**. There are 150 species in the cuckoo **family**. They live in woods and orchards throughout most of the world. Cuckoos have a long, rounded tail. Some species of cuckoo raise their own young in **nests** that they build in trees. Other species lay their **eggs** in the nest belonging to a different species of bird. The cuckoos leave the eggs to be hatched and looked after by the other bird.

curassow *noun*
Curassows are large **birds**. There are about 44 species in the curassow **family**. They live in the tropical **forests** of Central America, South America and southern North America. Curassows range in colour from deep blue to black. Their head has a curly crest and colourful knobs and flaps of skin called wattles. Curassows are poor fliers and spend most of their time on the ground, feeding mainly on fruit. Young curassows can leave the nest after only a few hours.

cuscus *noun*
Cuscuses are **mammals**. They are found in Australia, New Guinea and nearby islands. Cuscuses have big eyes, and tiny ears which are nearly hidden in the fur. They are **marsupials** and the young are carried in the mother's pouch until they develop. They spend most of their time in trees. Cuscuses are most active at night. They feed mainly on leaves and fruit but they also prey on lizards and birds.

courtship *noun*

Courtship is the way animals behave when they are ready to **mate** and want to attract a partner. Some animals show bright **colours** to members of the opposite sex. Others make loud sounds, produce strong smells or perform complicated dances. It is usually the male animal which courts the female.

court *verb*

The male fiddler crab waves his huge, colourful claw as a signal to female crabs.

The male blue bird of paradise gives one of the most spectacular of all courtship displays. He hangs upside down from a branch, opens his wings and spreads his tail. He then shakes his feathers and calls loudly to a female bird nearby.

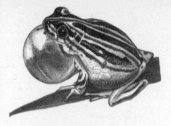

This male frog has blown up a huge pouch of air in his throat. His loud, bellowing cry will attract female frogs.

This female baboon has a bright red swelling around her tail. This shows that she is ready to mate and it attracts the male baboons in her group.

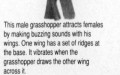

This male grasshopper attracts females by making buzzing sounds with his wings. One wing has a set of ridges at the base. It vibrates when the grasshopper draws the other wing across it.

A courting peacock bows to the female peahen. He opens his tail and struts up and down in front of her. He shakes his tail and rattles the feathers.

cuttlefish   *noun*
Cuttlefish are **molluscs**. There are about
100 species of cuttlefish. They are found in
most **oceans**, except around the Americas.
Cuttlefish have a support inside their body,
eight short arms and two longer arms, called
tentacles. All the arms and the tentacles
have rows of suckers, which are used for
catching **prey.** Their prey includes
crustaceans and small fish. If they are
threatened, cuttlefish release a dark, inky
cloud into the water. This contains a
pigment called sepia.

D

daddy longlegs   *noun*
Daddy longlegs are **arachnids**. They are
found in temperate countries and in the
tropics. Daddy longlegs have long, thin legs
and a small body. They eat small insects.

damselfly   *noun*
Damselflies are flying **insects** that live near
water. They are very similar to **dragonflies**.
When they are resting, damselflies hold their
wings together, but dragonflies spread out
their wings horizontally.

darter   *noun*
Darters are large water **birds**. The four
species of darter live in **freshwater** habitats
in **tropical** and subtropical parts of the
world. Darters have shiny, black **plumage**,
with silver on the back of their wings and
long neck. Their tail is long, broad and
tipped with brown. Darters are expert
swimmers and divers. They use their long,
sharp bill to spear fish and other prey under
the water.

deer   *noun*
Deer are **mammals**. There are more than
60 species of deer found on every continent
except Antarctica. They live mainly in
wooded areas, but some make their home in
tundra, **grassland** and **mountain** regions.
Deer have a short, smooth coat, long,
slender legs, and **hoofs**. Male deer are the
only animals with bones called antlers on
their head. Deer are **ruminants**. They feed
on leaves, flowers, grasses and twigs.

defence ► page 42

den *noun*
A den is an animal home used by **wolves**, **foxes** and **bears**. A den can be in a cave, a hollow log or under the ground. The animals use the den as a safe place for their young to grow. Wolves and foxes usually take over and enlarge **burrows** which have been abandoned by other animals.

desert *noun*
Desert is land that is very hot and dry and where few plants grow. The largest desert is the Sahara, in northern Africa. Some animals have **adapted** to living with little water. They get most of their water from their food. Some of these animals are **nocturnal** and are active at night when it is cool. About a fifth of all the Earth's land is desert.

digestion *noun*
Digestion occurs when food is broken down and absorbed inside the body. Most animals take in food through their **mouth**. It is digested in the **abdomen** and gut, and useful food parts are carried to the rest of the body. Waste food is then passed out through the **anus**.
digest *verb*

dik-dik *noun*
Dik-diks are **mammals**. They belong to the **bovid** family. The five species of dik-dik live in wooded areas in Africa. Dik-dik are small **antelopes**. They feed on shrubs.

dingo *noun*
The dingo is the wild **dog** of Australia. It has a pointed face, sharp, erect ears and a bushy tail. Dingoes usually have yellowish-brown **fur**. They were brought to Australia thousands of years ago by Aborigines, the first people to live in Australia. Dingoes live in family groups, but sometimes hunt together in large packs. **Wallabies** are their main food, but farmers think of them as **pests** because they also kill sheep.

dinosaur ► page 44

dipper *noun*
Dippers are small **birds**. There are five species in the dipper **family**. They live beside clear, running water in the hills and **mountains** of North America, South America, Europe, North Africa and Asia. Dippers have a round, dark-coloured body and a short tail. They feed on aquatic insects and **larva** which they find in the rivers. They can walk on the bottom of streams and can stay underwater for as long as 30 seconds.

display ► courtship

diver *noun*
Divers are **birds**. There are four species of diver. Divers are found in North America, northern Europe and northern Asia. They live on remote lakes and rivers in the warm **season**. Most **migrate** to the sea in the cold season. Divers have a streamlined body and strong legs and feet specially made for diving. They are expert swimmers and divers but cannot walk properly on land. They have a long, sharp bill which they use to catch fish and other water creatures.

dodo *noun*
The dodo was a large **bird** which died out, or became **extinct**, about 1680. It had tiny wings, short legs and a huge **bill**. It could not fly. Dodos lived in Mauritius and were related to **pigeons**. Sailors from Europe killed dodos for food. Pigs and monkeys, brought to Mauritius during the 1500s, destroyed dodo **eggs** and ate the young.

defence *noun*

Defence is the actions an animal takes to
protect itself from being caught and eaten.
The best defence is to hide from a **predator**.
Some animals are **camouflaged** and are not
easily seen. Other animals have a protective
covering or shell, so that they cannot be
attacked. When some animals are attacked
by a predator, they may try to scare the
predator or confuse it.

defend *verb*

The best defence is to run away. This
basilisk lizard lives near rivers and
when it is scared it runs over the
surface of the water. The scales on the
sides of its toes help it stay afloat.

When it is scared, the pufferfish
swallows lots of water or air and swells
up until it is almost round. This species
also has spikes which stick out.

This grass snake is pretending to be
dead. Most predators will not eat
carrion or dead animals. Even if the
snake is turned the right way up, it will
roll over again.

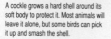

A cockle grows a hard shell around its soft body to protect it. Most animals will leave it alone, but some birds can pick it up and smash the shell.

When it is scared, this hawkmoth caterpillar can change its shape so that it looks like a small snake. The predator is scared of the snake and leaves it alone.

This spotted skunk is doing a handstand to show its bold black and white stripes. This is a warning to its attackers that it is about to squirt them with a nasty liquid.

The skink, along with some other species of lizard, has an unusual way of defending itself. When it is attacked, it breaks off its tail from its body. The predator eats the tail, while the skink runs away. The tail grows again.

dinosaur *noun*

Dinosaurs were animals which lived from
about 220 million years ago. About 63 million
years ago, dinosaurs vanished and are now
extinct. The name dinosaur means 'terrible
lizard'. Some dinosaurs were among the
largest animals that have ever lived on land.
Other dinosaurs were as small as a chicken.
Scientists do not know whether dinosaurs
were **cold-blooded** like reptiles, or **warm-
blooded** like mammals. Neither do scientists
know exactly why they disappeared.

The tyrannosaurus was the biggest meat-eating dinosaur.
It stood about seven metres high on its huge back legs. It
also had tiny front legs, but these did not even reach its
mouth. The tyrannosaurus had a large head with many
sharp teeth for tearing flesh of its prey.

The apatosaurus was one of the largest
dinosaurs. It was about 25 metres long.
It walked on its four heavy legs and ate
only plants. The apatosaurus had a
long tail and a long neck with a small
head.

The anatosaurus had a mouth like a duck. It ate plants by sucking in huge amounts of leaves and chewing them up with its hundreds of teeth.

The triceratops had three horns on its head and a large crest over its neck. These weapons helped the triceratops defend itself.

The stegosaurus had a row of large, horny plates along its back. Blood may have flowed through these plates and kept the stegosaurus cool. The sharp tail spikes were probably for defence.

This ankylosaurus is heavily armoured, with spikes of bone set into its leathery skin. The heavy, bony club at the end of the tail turned the tail into a powerful weapon.

dog *noun*
Dogs are **mammals**. They have long legs and a lean body. Wild species include **wolves**, **coyotes**, **foxes** and **jackals**. Wild dogs are found in every part of the world except New Zealand and some other islands. Dogs are intelligent and sociable and often live together in large groups. They are **carnivores** and often hunt for their prey in packs. They can run fast over long distances.

dogfish *noun*
Dogfish are **fish**. They are members of the **shark** order and there are about 70 species. They are found in the Atlantic Ocean and along the Pacific coast of North America. Dogfish have a long, slender body, large **fins** and a long tail. Most are less than two metres long. But the largest dogfish, the greenland shark, can grow as long as six metres. They are **carnivores** and eat small fish and other sea animals.

dolphin *noun*
Dolphins are sea **mammals**. There are 32 species in the dolphin **family**, which also includes the **killer whale** and pilot whale. Dolphins are found in all the **oceans**. Dolphins have a beaked snout and a body which is streamlined to slip easily through the water. They have two front **flippers** and a dorsal **fin** on their back. Dolphins come to the surface every few minutes to breathe air. Scientists think that dolphins may be one of the most intelligent animals.

domestic *adjective*
Domestic describes an animal species which people have tamed. People have tamed animals like **dogs** to help them hunt, or bullocks to help them pull heavy loads. People have tamed animals like sheep and chickens so they can use them for food.
domesticate *verb*

dominance *noun*
Dominance is used to describe animal behaviour when one animal shows itself to be stronger than another. An animal which shows its dominance wins food or mates. Dominance can be established by fighting between the animals. But sometimes the largest or most threatening animal can win without fighting.

dormouse *noun*
Dormice are tiny, furry **mammals**. There are 14 species of dormouse. They live in trees and bushes in Africa, Asia and Europe. Dormice have a fat body and a long tail which is usually bushy. They have fine, silky **fur** and large, black eyes. Dormice are **nocturnal** and search for nuts and berries at night. They build up a store of food when the weather starts to grow cold and **hibernate** through the cold **season**.

dorsal ► fish

down ► feather

dragonfly *noun*
Dragonflies are colourful, flying **insects** that live near water. They have four large, fine wings and huge, bulging eyes. Their body can be red, green or blue. Dragonflies are one of the fastest flying insects and can fly up to 97 kilometres an hour. They feed on other insects. The females lay their eggs in the water. The **nymphs** hatch within three weeks and may stay in the water for between 30 days and five or six years.

drone ► social insect

E

duck *noun*
Ducks are **birds**. The duck **family** includes **swans** and geese. Ducks live in marshes, rivers, lakes and the sea throughout the world, except in Antarctica. They have webbed feet and waterproof feathers. Many species of duck **migrate** long distances every year. Ducks feed on small water creatures and plants. Baby ducks can swim, run and find food a day and a half after **hatching** out of the egg.

dugong *noun*
The dugong is a rare sea **mammal**. It lives in the warm coastal waters around the Indian Ocean. The dugong has a large but streamlined body, and grows up to three metres long. Its snout is fleshy and rounded. Dugongs are shy, quiet animals. They spend most of their time lying on the sea-bed, rising to the surface to breathe every couple of minutes. Dugongs are **herbivores**, grazing mainly on seaweed and sea grass. They are a protected species, but people still hunt them for their skin, oil and meat.

duiker *noun*
Duikers are **mammals**. The three species live in Africa. The bay duiker and the yellow duiker inhabit dense **forests**, but the common duiker can live in almost any type of **habitat**. Like **goats**, duikers are members of the **bovid** family. Duikers have a smooth, glossy coat, slender legs and small horns on their head. They eat plants and sometimes snakes, eggs and chicks.

eagle *noun*
Eagles are large **birds** of prey. There are 60 species of eagle, found throughout the world except in Antarctica. Eagles have a hooked **bill**, powerful, curved **talons** and long wings. They rely on their sharp eyesight to hunt for food, sometimes from high up in the sky. Eagles build a nest of sticks, called an eyrie. They use the same nest each year but keep adding more sticks. Some eyries can be nearly three metres across and four and a half metres deep. Most eagles stay with the same mate for life.

ear ► page 48

earthworm *noun*
Earthworms are **invertebrates**. There are about 1,800 species of earthworm, and they are found in soil throughout the world. They usually live near the surface, but sometimes dig deep tunnels underground. Earthworms have a smooth body which is divided into many segments. They have a mouth but no eyes or ears. They breathe through their skin. Earthworms are **hermaphrodites**, so they are both male and female. They feed on dead plant material in the soil.

echo-location *noun*
Echo-location is a means of finding objects. It is used by some animals, such as **whales** and **porpoises**, to locate prey. Some animals, such as **bats**, also use echo-location to find their way around. The animal lets out a shrill noise and listens to the echo. This tells it if there is an object in front and how far away it is.

ear *noun*

Ears are the parts of an animal's body which it uses to hear sound. Sounds travel as waves. Ears pick up these waves and pass them as electrical messages to the brain. Animals' ears also help them balance. Each ear has sensitive hairs inside which change position when the animal moves.

This bat has big ears because it finds its way and its prey by echo-location. It sends out squeaks which bounce off objects and return as echoes.

Most mammals have a pair of ear flaps on the outside of the body. They are the only animals to have ear flaps. The African elephant has the largest ears of any animal. They are more than one metre across. The ears have many tiny blood vessels. These lose heat to the air and this keeps the elephant cool.

Insects, such as this cricket, do not
have true ears. But they can pick up
sound waves with delicate hairs on
their legs or stomach. The cricket has
hairs on its front pair of legs.

Amphibians, such as this frog, have a
circle of membrane behind each eye.
These are the eardrums. They pick up
sound waves and pass them to
hearing organs inside the head. One of
these organs recognizes the call of
frogs of the same species.

Birds can hear sounds higher than a
human can hear. This owl has more
accurate hearing than most birds,
because it hunts at night and must
hear its prey rather than see it. Each
ear is at a different height on the owl's
head. The owl can work out accurately
where a sound is coming from.

ecology   *noun*

Ecology is the study of an **environment**.
It includes all the relationships between
animals and plants and the area where they
live. Someone who studies ecology is called
an ecologist. Ecologists often study changes
in an area. They may find out how a change
in one animal's behaviour may affect many
other animals and plants.

ecosystem   *noun*

An ecosystem is all the living things that are
found in an area or **environment**. It includes
all the parts of the environment, such as the
rocks, the soil and the air. Energy moves
round and round the ecosystem in a **food
chain**.

eel   *noun*

Eels are long, slender **fish**. There are about
600 species of eel, found all over the world
except in polar regions. Most live in the
oceans, but some are found in fresh water.
Some species live in rivers and streams but
migrate to sea water to breed. Eels have a
dorsal **fin** along the whole of their back.
They feed on crustaceans, fish and insects.

egg ► page 51

electric eel   *noun*

An electric eel is a long, thin **fish**. It is not a
true **eel**. It lives in muddy streams and rivers
in South America where it feeds on fish and
frogs. The electric eel has three pairs of
electric **organs** on each side of its body
which produce an electric charge. The shock
can measure up to 650 volts. The electric
eel uses the electric charge to kill prey, for
defence and to help it navigate.

elephant   *noun*

Elephants are the largest **mammals** that live
on land. There are two species of elephant,
one in Africa, and the other in Asia. They are
found in **forests** and grassy **plains** where
they live in family groups called herds.
Elephants have a huge head, large ears,
ivory tusks and a long, flexible trunk. The
trunk is used for breathing, smelling, eating,
drinking and for picking up objects. Their
tusks are long teeth which they use to dig for
food and to fight. Elephants are **herbivores**
and feed on plants and fruits.

embryo   *noun*

The embryo is the earliest stage in the
growth of an animal. The embryo forms after
fertilization has taken place. In **mammals**,
the embryo grows inside the mother's body.
It is fed by an organ called the placenta until
it is ready to be born. In other animals, the
embryo grows in an **egg** outside the
mother's body. The embryo feeds on the
yolk of the egg until it is ready to hatch.

emu   *noun*

The emu is a large **bird**. The single **species**
of emu is found in Australia. It has long legs,
a long neck and brown, untidy-looking
feathers. It can grow as tall as two metres
and can run at a speed of 48 kilometres per
hour. The emu cannot fly. It wanders from
place to place, feeding on fruit, berries and
insects.

egg *noun*

An egg is a rounded or oval body produced
by a female animal. When an egg is
fertilized, it joins with the **sperm** from the
male parent. This produces an **embryo** of a
young animal. In most animals, including
birds, reptiles and fish, the female lays the
eggs outside the body. These eggs have
tough shells. The embryo grows inside the
egg until it is ready to **hatch**. In mammals,
the fertilized egg grows into a baby animal.

The female giant clam lays up to 1,000
million eggs at one time. This is more
than any other animal.

The tiny hummingbird's egg is less
than a centimetre long.

Ostriches lay the biggest bird's eggs in
the world. They can be 15 centimetres
long. They have tough shells that can
hold the weight of a human without
breaking.

The only function of the giant queen
termite is to lay eggs. Her huge, bloated
body is full of eggs.

eye *noun*

The eye is the part of the body which animals use to see. The simplest animals have eyes which pick up only patterns of light and dark. Other animals can see an accurate picture of what is in front of them. Light from air or water enters the eye and is focused by the lens onto the retina as an upside-down image. The brain turns the image the right way round. Some animals, particularly birds, can see better than humans. Other animals, such as **bees**, can see colours which humans cannot see.

Most invertebrates have simple eyes. These can only see light and dark. A scallop has a row of small, bright eyes. These can only see light, but the scallop can see when something is moving and it can escape.

The chameleon can move its eyes in different directions. This allows it to look forwards and backwards at the same time.

This dragonfly, like most insects and crustaceans, has both simple eyes and compound eyes. A compound eye is made up of many tiny eyes. The insect sees thousands of little images, which add up to one overall picture.

A rabbit has eyes on the side of its head. Each eye can see right around that side of the head, so it can spot predators. At the front and the back, the rabbit can see with both eyes. This is called stereoscopic vision.

A falcon has both eyes at the front of its head. The falcon sees with stereoscopic vision. This allows it to judge distances accurately. This is important when it is diving on its prey.

The tarsier has very large eyes. It is a nocturnal animal so it needs to see in dim light. Its big eyes help it pick up as much light as possible.

Animals which live in the dark may not have eyes at all, or they have tiny eyes. This cavefish lives inside a dark cave. It has lost the use of its eyes. It uses other senses to move around and hunt for food.

endangered species ► **rare**

endoskeleton *noun*
An endoskeleton is a **skeleton** which is found inside an animal and is covered entirely by a layer of flesh and an outer skin. All **vertebrates** have endoskeletons. The opposite of endoskeleton is **exoskeleton**.

environment *noun*
The environment is the area where an animal lives. This includes the living things, such as other animals and the plants, as well as the non-living things like sunlight, the soil and the weather. All these conditions can affect the animal. If an animal's environment is harmed or destroyed, the animal may become **rare** or die out.
environmental *adjective*

enzyme *noun*
Enzymes are chemical substances that are found in all living things. They help chemical changes in an animal's body happen many thousands of times faster. Without enzymes, life would not be possible. Animals have different kinds of enzymes which do different jobs. For example, some kinds help an animal to breathe, while others help it to digest food.

eohippus *noun*
Eohippus was a small, hoofed **mammal** that lived about 55 million years ago. It is now **extinct**. Eohippus fossils have been found in North America and Europe. They show that the eohippus stood between 25 and 50 centimetres high, and that it had an arched back and padded feet. It had four hoofs on the front feet, and three on the back.

estuary *noun*
An estuary is the area of land and water at the mouth of a river. Tides reach into an estuary and mix salt water with the fresh water of the river. Sea water may also flood the land as the tide comes in. Many kinds of sea **birds** and **waders** live in estuaries.

evolution *noun*
Evolution describes the very gradual changes that take place in the bodies of animals and plants. These changes may happen over thousands of years. During that time, a species may develop a new **characteristic**. It may grow taller than others of the same species. This characteristic is then passed on to the animal's offspring. For example, a horse today is about 150 centimetres tall, yet some scientists believe it evolved from the **eohippus** which was less than 50 centimetres tall.
evolve *verb*

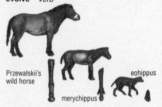

Przewalskii's wild horse

merychippus

eohippus

excrement ► **feces**

excrete *verb*
To excrete is to pass out or expel waste products from the body. All animal activity produces waste materials. Eating produces **feces** and moving can produce sweat. The animal must excrete these or it will die. Waste gases can be excreted from the **lungs**, through the skin or from the **anus**. In tiny organisms, waste is excreted through the cell **membrane**.
excretion *noun*

exoskeleton *noun*
An exoskeleton is a hard shell that covers animals such as **insects**, **crustaceans** and **tortoises**. It protects the animal and gives it its shape. Most exoskeletons do not grow with the animal, so the animal must regularly **moult** as it grows. The opposite of exoskeleton is **endoskeleton**.

extinct *adjective*
An extinct animal is one that does not exist
any more. Animals can become extinct if
they cannot **adapt** to a change in their
environment. The animals may all die, or
they may **evolve** into a different species.
Rare animals are ones which are in danger
of becoming extinct.
extinction *noun*

eye ► page 52

F

falcon *noun*
Falcons are medium-sized **birds**. There are
40 species in the falcon **family** including
kestrels, hobbies and merlins. Falcons are
found in many different **habitats** throughout
the world. They have long, pointed **wings**, a
strong, hooked **bill** and sharp, curved
talons. They are **birds of prey** that use their
sharp eyesight to hunt by day. Falcons are
spectacular and powerful fliers, often
plunging from a great height to catch small
animals.

family *noun*
A family is part of the system of
classification which scientists use to sort
animals. Family is the group which is smaller
than an **order**. For example, tigers, jaguars
and wild cats are all members of the **cat**
family. Each family is made up of smaller
groups, each called a **genus**.

fauna *plural noun*
Fauna describes all the animals that live in a
particular area. For example, the fauna of
Antarctica include seals, polar bears and
penguins. It also describes the animals that
lived at a particular time in the past. For
example, **dinosaurs** were part of the Earth's
fauna 100 million years ago.

feather ► page 56

feces *plural noun*
Feces are the solid waste matter that is
passed out, or expelled, from the **anus** of an
animal. This waste is what is left after the
rest of the food has been **digested**.

feather *noun*

A feather is a kind of fluffy hair. Feathers are light and flat and grow all over a bird's body. All birds have feathers. They keep the bird warm and those on the **wings** allow the bird to fly. Feathers can be many **colours**. The colouring can be used to **camouflage** the bird or as display in **courtship**. Feathers are dead. They are made of a hard protein called keratin, like nails, hair and reptiles' scales. Feathers wear out, so many birds **moult** and grow a new set at least once a year.

Wing feathers are the strong, shaped feathers which the bird uses to fly. Some birds change direction when they are flying by fanning out these feathers.

A feather has a main shaft with small shafts, or barbs, branching out from it. Tiny bristles called barbules branch off each barb. The bristles have hooked ends which grip each other and lock the feathers tightly together.

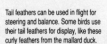

Tail feathers can be used in flight for steering and balance. Some birds use their tail feathers for display, like these curly feathers from the mallard duck.

Body feathers cover most of the bird's body and wings. They are short, compact feathers, with a layer of down next to the skin. Most feathers are waterproof. This duck must oil its feathers so that the water cannot reach its body.

Down feathers are the short, soft feathers found on baby birds. Adult birds also have a layer of down feathers next to their skin, to keep them warm.

mallard duck

wing feathers

tail feathers

down feathers

body feathers

feeler   *noun*
A feeler is an **antenna**. Most insects have a
pair of feelers on their head. A feeler can
also refer to a **tentacle**. Feelers are
sensitive to touch.

female   *adjective*
Female describes those animals which
produce eggs or young. The opposite of
female is **male**. Some animals, such as a
snail, can be both female and male.
They are called **hermaphrodite**.

feral   *adjective*
Feral describes an individual animal or a
species of animal which was once
domesticated. It now lives in the wild.
Many pet cats become feral when they are
abandoned by their owners.

ferret   *noun*
A ferret is a small **mammal**. It is a member
of the **weasel** family. The black-footed ferret
is the only wild species and lives on the
plains in North America. It has a long, thin
body, short legs and a long tail. It can run
extremely fast. Ferrets are **carnivores**, and
feed mainly on **prairie dogs**. However, there
are very few prairie dogs left on the plains
and wild ferrets now face extinction. Another
species of ferret is **domesticated** and kept
as a pet.

fertile   *adjective*
Fertile describes an animal that can produce
young. The opposite of fertile is **infertile**.
fertility   *noun*

fertilize   *verb*
Fertilize describes the joining of the **egg**
from the female animal and the **sperm** from
the male animal. When the egg is fertilized
by the sperm, a young animal starts to grow.
Fertilization is the first stage in **sexual
reproduction**.
fertilization   *noun*

fin   *noun*
A fin is a flat flap which sticks out from the
body of a **fish**, or animals such as **dolphins**
and **whales**. Fish can move their fins and
they use them for swimming, balancing and
changing direction in the water. Fins are
made of many small spines joined by a band
of skin.

fin

finch   *noun*
Finches are small **birds**. They are found in
wooded areas in most parts of the world.
Finches use to feed on seeds, fruit and nuts. Some
species also eat insects and worms. Many
species, such as the canary, have a
melodious, warbling song.

fish ► page 60

flagellate   *noun*
A flagellate is a tiny **organism** that is made
up of only one cell. It is so small that it can
only be seen through a powerful
microscope. A flagellate belongs to a group
of living things called **protista**. It is a
protozoa with a long, thin tail called a
flagellum. It waves its tail to move around.
Flagellates live in any moist place and can
even live inside plants or animals. Some
flagellates are green. They make their food
as plants do, using energy from the Sun.

flamingo *noun*
Flamingos are large, pink or
pinkish-white **birds**. There
are five **species** in the
flamingo **family**. They are
found near lakes, marshes
and seas, mainly in South
America, Africa and Asia.
Flamingos have a long,
curved neck, large **wings**
and very long legs with
webbed feet. They live in
huge **colonies**. Flamingos
feed in water. With their
large, curved bill upside-
down, they filter out small
creatures from the sand
and gravel.

flatfish *noun*
Flatfish are **fish**. There are over 500 species
of flatfish found throughout the world. Most
live in **oceans**, but a few are found in **fresh
water**. Flatfish live on the sea-bed, often
buried in sand or mud. When they are
young, flatfish are the same shape as other
species of fish. But as they develop, one
eye moves closer to the other eye until
both eyes are on the same side of their
head. The flatfish then swim or lie on one
side. The side which has the eyes is always
facing upwards. Flatfish eat worms,
crustaceans and other fish.

flatworm *noun*
Flatworms are **invertebrates**. There are
about 17,000 species of flatworm, including
tapeworms and **flukes**. Some species live
in sand and mud on the bottom of **ocean**
and **freshwater** habitats and some live in
moist soil on land. Other species are
parasites and live in animals or humans.
Flatworms have a flat body and are usually
less than two and a half centimetres long.
But some species can grow very long,
up to 30 metres. Most flatworms are
hermaphrodites, which means they are
both male and female.

flea *noun*
Fleas are small, wingless **insects**. They live
on **mammals** and **birds**, feeding on their
blood. Some kinds of flea live only on one
species of animal, but most pass from one
species to another. Fleas have a flat body,
a small head and powerful legs. They can
jump up to 200 times the length of their
body. Fleas are **pests** and many carry
germs that cause disease.

flight *noun*
Flight is the movement of animals through
the air. Most birds, bats and insects can fly.
They have **wings** and can control their flight.
Other animals, such as flying squirrels,
can glide through the air. They have flaps of skin
which act like a parachute.
fly *verb*

flipper *noun*
A flipper is a broad, flat front leg used for
swimming. **Turtles**, and **mammals** such as
seals that live in the sea, have flippers. The
small wings of **penguins** are called flippers.

fluke *noun*
Flukes are **invertebrates**. They are a
species of **flatworm** and are found
throughout the world. Flukes are **parasites**
and live in the blood, intestine, liver and
lungs of animals and people. Flukes have a
flat, often leaf-shaped body, but they can
also be round or long. They have suckers
and hooks underneath their body which they
use to attach themselves to their **host**.

fly *noun*
Flies are small **insects**. There are about
100,000 species of fly, found throughout the
world. Flies have two pairs of wings, only
one of which they use for flying. The two
back wings are like small sticks and are
used to balance. A fly's mouth is a long tube,
called a **proboscis**, which it uses to suck up
liquids. There are four stages in the
metamorphosis of a fly. These are egg,
larva, pupa and adult.

fish *noun*

A fish is a **vertebrate** that lives all its life in water. Fish make up four **classes** of animals and scientists have named nearly 22,000 species. Fish breathe under water through their **gills**. A fish's **scaly** body is tapered at both ends, and has **fins** which help it to swim. Most fish contain a bubble of air called the **swim bladder**, which helps them to stay afloat. Many fish have **skeletons** made of **bone**. These are called **bony fish**. Fish with skeletons made of **cartilage** are called **cartilaginous fish**. Fish are **cold-blooded**. They live anywhere there is water.

Most fish, such as trout, lay eggs or spawn once a year. Some male fish attract the female by courtship. When the fish are paired, they reproduce by sexual reproduction.

nostril

eye

scales

dorsal fin

tail

mouth

gill

pectoral fin

pelvic fin

lateral line system

This is an adult trout.

The female fish lays large numbers of soft eggs. The male drops his sperm which fertilize the eggs. The parents then abandon the eggs. The female trout covers the eggs first. In some fish, the eggs are fertilized inside the female's body.

The baby fish, or embryo, grows inside the egg. It feeds on the egg yolk.

When a young fish hatches, it continues to feed on the yolk. Young fish do not receive any care from their parents and must look after themselves.

This young trout is old enough to hunt for its food. It still looks like a young fish, but it will become more like an adult as it grows. Most young fish are eaten by predators before they become adults.

flycatcher *noun*
Flycatchers are **birds**. There are two
families of flycatcher. One family lives in
North America and South America. Many
birds in this family catch insects while in
flight. The other family lives in Europe,
Africa, Asia and Australia. Many birds in this
family perch on a branch while they wait for
their **prey**. When an insect flies past, the
birds dart out and snatch it, returning to the
perch to eat.

flying fish *noun*
Flying fish are **fish**. There are over
50 species of flying fish and they are found
throughout the world in warm **oceans**. Flying
fish have either two or four fins that look like
wings and which help them to fly. Flying fish
swim fast in the water, and then use their
strong tail fins to launch themselves above
the surface. Once in the air, they spread
their wings and can glide as far as
300 metres. They often leave the water
to escape from **predators**.

flying lemur *noun*
A flying lemur is a **mammal**. There are two
species of flying lemur, which are found in
forests in South-east Asia. They are not
really able to fly, but can use the skin, or
membrane, stretched between their feet
and the length of their body to glide through
the air. Flying lemurs are hardly able to walk
on the ground, but they climb well. They are
nocturnal animals and spend the day
hanging from branches. At night, they glide
from tree to tree feeding on buds, leaves,
fruit and flowers.

food chain *noun*
The food chain is the cycle of food energy
which is passed from one living thing to
another. Plants are at the bottom of the food
chain. A plant is eaten by a **herbivorous**
animal, such as a fish. This animal is then
eaten by a **carnivorous** animal, such as a
seal. This carnivorous animal may then be
eaten by another animal, such as a polar
bear.

foot ► page 62

forest *noun*
Forests are large areas of land covered with
trees and other plants. There are different
types of forest throughout the world.
Temperate forests are found in Asia, Europe
and North America. Many different species
of bird, insect and mammal live in temperate
forests. Large mammals such as **bears** and
deer can be found here. **Tropical** forests are
found near the Equator where the weather is
hot and humid. Some of these forests are
rain forests.

fossil *noun*
Fossils are the remains of living things, or
organisms, that have been preserved in
rocks. These organisms lived thousands or
millions of years ago. Scientists study fossils
to find out about animals that are now
extinct, such as the **archeopteryx** and the
eohippus. Fossils can also show how
animals have **evolved**.

fox *noun*
Foxes are **mammals**. There are about
10 species of fox, which belong to the **dog**
family. Foxes are found in a variety of
habitats, in all parts of the world except
Antarctica and South-east Asia. Foxes have
pointed ears, a bushy tail and a long, narrow
snout. They are **carnivores** and feed on
mice, rabbits, birds and **carrion**. They
usually hunt at night. Foxes rear their young
in **dens**. Most use **burrows** abandoned by
other animals.

foot (plural **feet**)   *noun*

A foot is a part of an animal's body. An animal
stands on its feet. Some invertebrates, such
as **millipedes**, have many feet. Vertebrates
have no more than four feet. Birds and
people stand on two feet. Most animals have
toes on their feet. Some, such as **ungulates**,
walk on their toes. The toes of ungulates are
covered with a hard hoof.

The long, flat part of a snail is its foot.
Wave movements through the foot push
the snail forward.

The mountain goat is an ungulate.
Its hoofs have a hard rim with a soft,
spongy pad inside. These allow the
goat to grip onto rough rocks or ice.
Mountain goats climb high into the
mountains and can walk on tiny ledges.

This gecko has special scales on its
feet. These allow the gecko to grip
vertical surfaces. A gecko can even run
upside down.

Kangaroos have very different front and
back feet. They run by pushing off with
their long back feet. They use their front
paws when they are walking.

A jacana is a bird with very large feet
and widely spaced toes. It is light
enough to walk on leaves on water.

fragmentation   *noun*
Fragmentation is a form of **asexual reproduction**. Some **worms** reproduce by fragmentation. In fragmentation, an animal splits into two or more parts. Each part then develops into a new adult.

freshwater crayfish ► crayfish

freshwater habitat   *noun*
A freshwater habitat is an area of water that is not salty. Fresh water is found in all parts of the world. Rivers, streams and lakes are all freshwater habitats. Many species of fish, insect and amphibian live in fresh water, for example, **guppies**, water **beetles** and **frogs**. The **oceans** are saltwater habitats.

frigate bird   *noun*
Frigate birds are large sea **birds**. The five species of frigate bird are found in all the tropical **oceans**. Frigate birds have long, pointed **wings** and a forked tail. Their black **plumage** has a metallic sheen. Some frigate birds have a white stomach. During **courtship**, male frigate birds grow a red pouch under their bill. They blow the pouch up like a balloon to attract females. When they are not breeding in **colonies** on remote islands, frigate birds spend their time at sea, feeding on fish.

frog   *noun*
Frogs are small **amphibians** and are found throughout the world, except Antarctica. Most species live in or near fresh water. Others live on land, in trees or in underground **burrows**. Frogs have bulging eyes and no tail. They use their long, strong back legs for jumping and swimming. Nearly all frogs breed in water. Males have a loud call which they use to attract a mate. Frogs feed on insects, worms and rodents. There are three stages in the development, or **metamorphosis**, of a frog. These are egg, tadpole and adult frog.

fur   *noun*
Fur is the hair that covers the body of many **mammals**. It keeps the animal warm and protects the skin from damage. **Rabbits**, **beavers**, **apes** and bears all have fur.

G

gannet *noun*
Gannets are large, white **birds**. There are
nine species in the gannet **family**, including
the **booby**. They live on nearly all the
world's **oceans**. Gannets have short legs
and long, pointed, black-tipped wings. The
wings can be up to 1.8 metres in width. They
spend most of their time at sea, only coming
to shore to breed in **colonies**. There can be
up to 50,000 gannets in a colony. Female
gannets lay one egg in a nest of seaweed.
Gannets dive into the water for their food of
fish and squid.

gavial *noun*
A gavial is a **reptile**. It is found in large
rivers in north India, and spends most of its
time in the water. The gavial looks like a
crocodile but has a long, narrow **snout**.
It moves its snout from side to side to
catch fish. It grows about six metres long.
The female leaves the water to lay more
than 40 eggs in a **nest**. The gavial is very
rare and is in danger of extinction.

gazelle *noun*
Gazelles are graceful **mammals** that are
noted for their gentleness. There are about
15 species of gazelle, which are members of
the **bovid** family. They live in herds that
wander over the open **plains** of Asia and
northern and eastern Africa. A few species
live in mountain regions. Gazelles have
horns, slender legs, hoofed feet, and long,
narrow ears. They are fast runners. Gazelles
are **herbivores** and eat grass, berries and
leaves. About 10 species of gazelle have
now become **rare**.

gecko *noun*
Geckos are small **reptiles**. They are a
species of **lizard**. Geckos are found in a
variety of **habitats**, such as **forests** and
deserts, in warm parts of the world. They
have large eyes, soft skin and a fragile tail.
The tail can break off when a gecko is
attacked. Geckos have pads on their feet
that help them to cling to surfaces when they
are climbing. They are **insectivores** and
usually feed at night. Most geckos make
loud calls.

genera ► **genus**

genet *noun*
Genets are **mammals**. They belong to the
civet family, and live in the **forests** and
grasslands of Africa, Asia and Europe.
Genets have a long body, short legs, a
pointed nose and long tail. They are usually
pale yellow or grey, with dark stripes and
spots. Genets are **carnivores** and feed on
rodents, birds and insects. They are
nocturnal and hunt at night. Genets live
alone or in pairs. They live mainly on the
ground but can climb trees.

genus (plural **genera**) *noun*
A genus is part of the system of animal
classification. Genus is the group which is
smaller than a **family**. Each genus is made
up of smaller groups called **species**.
Different species are very similar but
which have some differences, such as lions,
leopards and tigers, are members of the
same genus.

gerbil   *noun*
Gerbils are small, furry **mammals**. There are
about 100 species of gerbil, found in
deserts, **plains** and **savanna** in Asia and
Africa. Gerbils are pale brown or grey in
colour and have a white belly. Most species
have long, hairy hind legs and feet and a
long tail. Gerbils are **rodents**. They are
herbivores and eat seeds, roots and other
plant material. They dig **burrows** and store
food in them. Some species of gerbil are
nocturnal. Female gerbils usually give birth
to four or five young, but some have as
many as 12.

gestation   *noun*
Gestation is the time when a young animal
is growing inside its mother's body.
Gestation begins when an **egg** is **fertilized**
and lasts until the baby animal is born.
Some animals have a long gestation. For
example, an elephant's gestation is
22 months. The brown bandicoot has a
gestation of only 11 days.

gibbon   *noun*
Gibbons are long-haired, tailless **mammals**.
There are six species of gibbon and they
belong to the ape family. They live in the
forests of Southeast Asia, and spend most
of their time in the trees. Gibbons have a
small body and long arms and legs. They
are very agile and use their long arms to
swing from branch to branch. Gibbons feed
on fruit, leaves, insects and young birds.
They live in small family groups, consisting
of the male, female and their **offspring**.

gila monster   *noun*
Gila monsters are **reptiles**. There are two
species in the gila monster family. They are
found in dry **habitats** near Central America.
Gila monsters have a stout body and a thick
tail. They are the only poisonous **lizards**.
Gila monsters live under rocks or in
burrows. They feed on small mammals,
birds and birds' eggs. They store fat in their
tail and can live on this for months without
eating.

gill   *noun*
A gill is the part of the body that most
underwater animals use for breathing. Most
fish have gills. **Molluscs**, **crustaceans** and
some underwater **insects** also have gills.
These animals swallow water and push it out
through the gills. In the feathery
membranes of the gill, oxygen passes from
the water into the blood.

giraffe   *noun*
A giraffe is a very tall **mammal**. It lives in
herds on the **savanna** in Africa. The giraffe
has long legs and a long neck. It has a light
coloured coat covered with dark spots. It is
the tallest animal, and can grow more than
five and a half metres tall. The giraffe is a
herbivore and feeds on the leaves, twigs
and fruits high up in trees and bushes. It can
go for many weeks without drinking. Giraffes
usually sleep standing up.

gland *noun*
A gland is a part of the body which gives out a useful substance. This substance affects the animal's body in a particular way. For example, glands can control **digestion** and can help keep the skin cool. Some glands produce **hormones**. These control such things as an animal's growth.

gnu *noun*
Gnus are large **mammals**. The two species of gnu belong to the **bovid** family which also includes bison and buffaloes. They are African **antelopes** that live in large herds on **grassland** and **savanna**. Gnus have long, curved horns, massive shoulders, and a large head. They are **herbivores** and eat leaves, twigs and grass. They need to drink frequently, so they stay close to water sources. During the dry season, herds of gnus **migrate** great distances to find water and food. Gnus are also called wildebeest.

goat *noun*
Goats are **mammals**. There are five **species** of wild goat and they belong to the **bovid** family. Wild goats are found in rocky and mountainous areas in Europe and Asia. Goats have horns, coarse fur and a short tail. The males usually have a beard. Goats are **ruminants** and feed on almost any vegetation, such as leaves, bushes and bark. The females, called does, and their young, live in herds and are only joined by the male during the mating season. There are also many species of **domestic** goat.

goose (plural **geese**) *noun*
Geese are large **birds**. They are members of the **duck** family. They are found mostly in Asia, North America and Europe. Geese have a sturdy body, long neck, short legs and webbed feet. They make a honking noise. Geese have waterproof **feathers** and are good swimmers, but they can also walk well on land. Geese **migrate** over long distances, flying north in the warm **season** and south in the cold season.

gopher *noun*
Gophers are small **mammals**. They live in North America. Gophers have short legs, small eyes and ears and a short tail. They have large, fur-lined pouches on their cheeks which they use to carry food. Gophers are **herbivores** and feed on roots, grass and nuts. Gophers live alone in complicated **burrows**, which they dig with their claws and their strong, front teeth. They only leave the burrow during the mating season and to find food.

gorilla *noun*
Gorillas are large **mammals**. They belong to the **ape** family. They live in small groups in **rain forests** in Central and West Africa. Gorillas have a large body covered with black hair, long arms and short legs. They sit upright but walk on all fours. Gorillas spend most of their time on the ground. They are **herbivores** and feed on leaves, fruits and bark. Male gorillas warn off rivals by roaring and beating their chest.

grasshopper *noun*
Grasshoppers are jumping **insects**. They are found in **grasslands** and **forests** in most parts of the world, except the polar regions. Grasshoppers either have long, thin **antennae** and are called long-horned, or have short antennae and are called short-horned. Most grasshoppers are **herbivores** and feed on plants and leaves, but a few eat insects. Male grasshoppers "sing" during **courtship**, by rubbing their legs together. Different species have different songs.

grassland *noun*
A grassland is a **habitat** where mainly
grasses grow, with only a few trees or
shrubs. Many large animals live on
grasslands, such as **elephants**, **kangaroos**
and **giraffes**. There are also very fast
predators, such as the **cheetah**. But most
grassland animals are small and not easily
noticed, like the **rodents**.

grebe *noun*
Grebes are water **birds**. There are 19
species of grebe, found all over the world.
Grebes have a flattened, streamlined body
and waterproof **feathers**. They have small
wings and short legs far back on their body.
They are hardly able to walk, but are expert
at swimming and diving. Grebes catch fish
and water snails under water.

grison *noun*
A grison is a small, agile **mammal**. There
are three species of grison, which are
members of the same family as **weasels**
and **martens**. Grisons live in the **forests**
and **plains** of Central and South America.
They have a long, thin body, a furry tail and
short legs. Their fur is grey, white and black.
Grisons are **carnivores**, and feed on worms,
frogs and other small animals. They often
make a den in the abandoned burrow of
another animal.

grouse *noun*
Grouse are plump **birds**. They are members
of the **pheasant** family, as are turkeys, quails
and guinea-fowl. Grouse are found in cooler
parts of North America, northern Europe and
Asia. They have dull-coloured **plumage** and
have **feathers** on their legs and short wings.

guard hair *noun*
Guard hairs are the thick hairs that form a
protective covering over the fine underfur of
many **mammals**. They often contain oil and
are waterproof. When the weather is cold or
wet, guard hairs trap warm air close to the
animal's skin.

guillemot *noun*
A guillemot is a large sea **bird**. There are
two species of guillemot, which belong to the
auk family. They live on the open waters and
along the coasts of the North Atlantic and
North Pacific oceans. Guillemots have a
short neck and tail, and a long, sharp bill.
Their plumage is dark brown, with white
underparts in winter.

guinea-fowl *noun*
Guinea-fowl are **birds**. They are members of
the **pheasant** family. There are seven
species of guinea-fowl, which all live in
Africa. Guinea-fowl have a heavy body, short
wings and a bare head with a crest of
feathers or a hard, bony helmet. They have
dark grey **plumage**, covered with small,
white spots. They feed on insects and plants.

guinea pig ► **cavy**

gull *noun*
Gulls are white sea **birds**. There are about
90 **species** of gull which are found all over
the world. They have black or grey
markings. Gulls live mainly near **oceans**, but
some make their homes near inland waters.
Terns are small, graceful members of the
gull **family**, which dive from the air into the
sea for fish. The Arctic tern has the longest
migration of any bird. Every year, it travels
15,000 kilometres from the Arctic to the
Antarctic, and back again.

H

guppy *noun*
Guppies are small, colourful **fish**. They are found in **freshwater** streams in Venezuela and the Caribbean islands. Adult males are about two and a half centimetres long. Females are larger than males, and are a dull, brown colour. Guppies feed on insect **larvae**, worms and small crustaceans. Unlike most species of fish, guppies do not lay eggs. They give birth to live young. About 30 to 50 young are born at one time.

habitat ► page 70

hagfish *noun*
Hagfish are long, slender **fish**. They live on the **sea-bed** of most **oceans** of the world. Hagfish have a thin mouth with six short **barbs**. Unlike most fish, they do not have a jaw, bones or scales and are almost blind. Hagfish feed on dead or dying fish. They have sharp teeth on their tongue which they use to chew into their **prey**. The hagfish then eat the flesh and leave the skin and bone. Hagfish are similar to **lampreys**.

hamster *noun*
Hamsters are small, furry **mammals**. There are 15 species of hamster, found in the **steppes** and **grasslands** of Europe and Asia. Hamsters have a stout body, a small tail and large cheek pouches for carrying food. They are **rodents**. Most species are **nocturnal**. They live alone in burrows that have separate chambers for sleeping and storing food. Hamsters are **omnivores** and feed on fruit, grain, vegetables, insects and small animals. Some species **hibernate** during the winter.

hare *noun*
Hares are small **mammals**. They are found in a variety of **habitats** throughout the world, except Australia and Antarctica. Hares have strong back legs, long, narrow ears and a small tail. Most are brownish-grey, but some hares that live in cold climates turn completely white in the cold **season** to stay **camouflaged** against the white snow. Hares are **herbivores** and are usually nocturnal.

habitat *noun*

A habitat is an area, such as a **desert** or an **ocean**, where an animal usually lives.
Some animals have **adapted** to live only in one habitat. For example, most
penguins can only live in cold oceans. Other animals can live in different
habitats. The **chamois** lives in the mountains in warm weather and
moves to forests in the valley when it is cold.
There are eight major habitats around the
world, including fresh water.

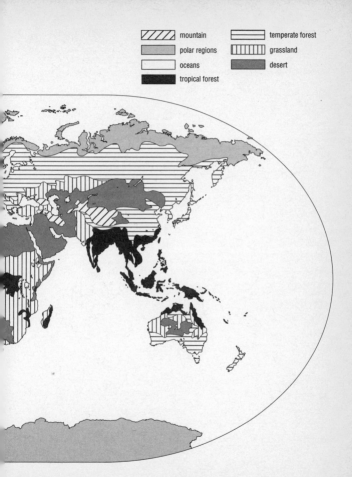

	mountain		temperate forest
	polar regions		grassland
	oceans		desert
	tropical forest		

hatch   *verb*

1. Hatch describes how an animal breaks out of its **egg** when it is fully grown. Many **birds** and **reptiles** break through the hard or leathery shell using a special knob on their nose called the egg tooth.

2. Hatch also describes the **incubation** of the egg by the parents.

hawk   *noun*

Hawks are **birds of prey**. They are found throughout the world, except in the polar regions. They vary greatly in size and appearance, but all have a pointed, down-curving bill, sharp, strong **talons** and large wings with rounded tips. Hawks feed on a wide variety of animals, such as reptiles, fish, insects and small mammals. They have very good eyesight and swoop down on their prey from high up in the air.

head   *noun*

The head is the front part of an animal. The head contains the **sense** organs, the mouth and the brain. In an **insect**, the main parts of the body are the head, the **abdomen** and the **thorax**.

hedgehog   *noun*

Hedgehogs are small **mammals**. They live in Asia, Europe, Africa and New Zealand. Hedgehogs have a round body, a small head and a pointed face. They have short, sharp spines covering their back. If in danger, a hedgehog rolls itself into a ball for defence. Hedgehogs are **nocturnal** and hunt for insects, birds, worms and snakes. Some species **hibernate** during the cold **season**.

herbivore   *noun*

A herbivore is an animal which eats only plants or seeds. Herbivores are well **adapted** for eating the coarse materials in plants. They may have strong, ridged **teeth** for grinding, like the animals in the **bovid** family, such as buffalo. Some herbivores, such as **giraffes**, are **ruminants**. They have a long stomach with four parts and chew their food a second time as cuds. Animals which eat only meat are called **carnivores** and those which eat both flesh and plants are called **omnivores**.

hermaphrodite   *noun*

A hermaphrodite is an animal which is both **male** and **female**. It produces both **eggs** and **sperm**. Some hermaphrodites **fertilize** their own eggs, but most do not. They **mate** with another animals of the same species. Some **flatworms**, and segmented **worms**, **barnacles** and **snails** are hermaphrodite.

hermit crab   *noun*

Hermit crabs are **invertebrates**. They live on the **sea-bed**, on the **sea-shore** and on land. Hermit crabs are **crustaceans**. They have a soft body and hard claws. To protect their body, they usually live in the empty shell of a sea snail. They can block the opening of the shell with their claws. When hermit crabs grow, they have to leave their shell to find a new, larger one. Some hermit crabs don't live in shells, but are found in holes in **coral**, rock or wood. Other kinds of hermit crab live most of their life on the shore. Hermit crabs are **carnivores**.

heron   *noun*

Herons are **birds**. There are about 60 species in the heron **family**, which also includes bitterns and egrets. They are found near inland water throughout the world, except in high areas. Herons have a slender body, long legs and neck, and large, wide wings. They catch their **prey** of fish and other water animals by snapping at them with their strong, dagger-like bill.

hibernation *noun*

Hibernation is a kind of deep sleep. Some animals hibernate during months of cold weather. During hibernation, the animal's breathing and heartbeat slow down and its body temperature falls to nearly zero degrees Celsius. The animal seems to be almost dead. Hibernation allows an animal to survive through cold weather, as it needs very little food. The animal always hibernates in a safe place.

hibernate *verb*

Some cold-blooded animals also hibernate. But they are easily woken from their sleep, so this is not true hibernation.

Some warm-blooded animals prepare for hibernation each year. They eat plenty of food to build up the fat in their bodies.

This bat is hibernating in a dark, dry cave. Only bats which live in temperate climates hibernate when the weather gets cold. In tropical areas, the climate stays warm enough for the bat to keep active.

This frog has buried itself in the mud at the bottom of a lake. The mud helps to protect it from the cold weather.

This ground squirrel has stored food in its burrow. It will wake up a few times during the cold weather, eat some food, then fall back into hibernation.

This snake is sheltering in a heap of dead leaves, under a rock.

This bear is hibernating in a warm den below the ground.

herring *noun*
Herrings are long **fish**. They have large, silvery scales. Herring is also the name of an **order** which includes sardines and anchovies. Herrings are found in the north Pacific and north Atlantic oceans. They swim in large groups, called schools, near the surface of the water. They feed on **plankton**.

hibernate ► page 73

hippopotamus *noun*
Hippopotamuses are large **mammals**. The two species of hippopotamus both live in Africa. They live in herds in lakes and rivers near **grassland**. Hippopotamuses have a barrel-shaped body, short, thick legs, a big head and a large mouth. They lie in the water with their body submerged, but their eyes, ears and nostrils remain above water. They can also walk along the bottom of the water and can run fast on land. They are **herbivores**.

hive ► social insect

hoatzin *noun*
The hoatzin is a **bird**. It lives in flocks on river banks and **marshes** in South America. Hoatzins have a long tail, large wings and feathers on their head. Young hoatzins are born with a pair of claws on their wings to help them climb trees. The claws fall off as the hoatzins grow and learn to fly. Hoatzins are **herbivores** and feed on leaves and fruits. They build their nests in trees over water.

hog ► pig

honeyeater *noun*
Honeyeaters are small **birds**. There are about 170 species of honeyeater. Nearly all live in Australia, southern Asia and islands in the Pacific Ocean. Honeyeaters have a long tail. They usually have a long, curved bill, shaped for drinking nectar from flowers. Honeyeaters also eat insects and fruit.

honeyguide *noun*
Honeyguides are small, dull-coloured **birds**. They are found in Africa, Asia and Indonesia. They get their name from their practice of leading mammals such as the **ratel** to bees' nests. The honeyguide sings and flies ahead of the animal, guiding it to the nest. When the animal breaks open the nest, the honeyguide feeds on the wax and **larvae** of the bees. It also eats other insects.

hoof *noun*
A hoof is the tough, horny covering on the foot of a group of mammals called **ungulates**. The hoof protects the foot. **Zebras**, **deer** and **antelopes** all have hoofs.

hookworm *noun*
Hookworms are **parasites** that live in the intestine of humans and some animals. They are small **roundworms** that feed on the blood of their **host**. They are found in **tropical** countries. Hookworms cause disease in the host.

hoopoe *noun*
A hoopoe is a pinkish-brown coloured **bird**. It lives in the warmer areas of Europe, Asia and Africa. The hoopoe has black and white wings and tail and a long crest of feathers on its head. It has a long, thin bill that curves downwards. It uses the bill to poke the ground to find insects and other small **invertebrates**. The hoopoe lives mainly on the ground. It makes nests in holes in trees and rocks. As the female **incubates** the eggs, the male hoopoe feeds her.

hormone *noun*
A hormone is a substance which an animal produces and which causes an effect in the animal's body. Most hormones are produced in **glands**. Hormones are carried in the blood. Hormones control changes such as growth, **reproduction** and the way the body uses its food. All animals produce hormones. For example, insects produce hormones which cause **moulting**.

horn *noun*
A horn is a bony stalk that grows on the head of some **mammals**. **Antelopes**, **rhinoceroses** and **goats** have horns. Horns are made of a bony core which is covered with a layer of skin. They can be curved or straight. Usually animals have a pair of horns. These last for life. Horns are used by animals for **defence** and for fighting.

hornbill *noun*
Hornbills are large **birds**. There are over 40 species of hornbill and most live in trees in Africa and tropical Asia. Hornbills usually have brown or black and white **plumage**. They have a huge bill with a horny lump on the top. The female hornbill closes herself into the nest after laying her eggs and stays there until the eggs hatch. The male feeds her through a slit. Then she breaks out when the chicks are old enough to mend the hole in the nest. The male and female then feed the chicks through the slit until they can fly.

horse ► **wild horse**

horseshoe crab *noun*
Horseshoe crabs are **invertebrates**. They are not true **crabs**. There are four species of horseshoe crab, which are found on the **sea-bed** on the east coasts of Asia and North America. Horseshoe crabs have a shell that covers the head, six pairs of legs, and a long, spiny 'tail'. The front pair of legs has pincers at the end to capture prey. The largest species of horseshoe crab grows over one metre long. Horseshoe crabs feed on worms and small **molluscs**. Fossil horseshoe crabs have been found that are over 130 million years old.

host *noun*
A host is a living thing in which or on which a **parasite** lives. Animals, plants and humans are hosts. **Dogs** and **monkeys** may be hosts to **fleas**. Humans may be hosts to **flukes**.

hummingbird *noun*
Hummingbirds are small **birds**. There are more than 300 species of hummingbird, found throughout North America and South America. Many hummingbirds have beautiful, jewel-like colours and a very long and slender bill. Their name comes from the humming sound made by the very fast beating of their wings. Hummingbirds can fly more expertly than any other bird. They can hover and even fly backwards.
Hummingbirds feed mainly on insects. Some species have a specially shaped bill to suck the nectar from flowers.

hyena *noun*

Hyenas are **mammals**. They live on the **plains**, **savanna** and **desert** in Africa and south-western Asia. Hyenas have a large head, a long snout and a sloping back. They have very strong jaws and teeth which can crush large bones. The largest and most common is the spotted or laughing hyena. It makes a loud, wailing noise that sounds as if it is laughing. Hyenas are **predators** and often hunt in packs. Their **prey** includes sheep, goats and zebras. They also feed on **carrion**.

hyrax *noun*

Hyraxes are small, furry **mammals**. There are seven species, found in Africa and south-western Asia. Hyraxes have short legs and a short tail. They have nails on their toes, and special pads on their feet that help them when they climb. Some live in groups on rocky hills and others live alone in trees. Hyraxes are **herbivores** and feed on leaves, grass, fruit and other plant material.

I

ibex *noun*

Ibex are medium-sized, hoofed **mammals**. They are a kind of wild **goat** and belong to the **bovid** family. They are found in mountains in Italy and Switzerland. Ibex are sure-footed and have a claw at the back of their feet to help them climb. They have long, curving horns and live in herds.

ibis *noun*

Ibises are wading **birds**. There are more than 20 species. That live in wetlands, **plains** and **savanna** in many countries throughout the world. The ibis is medium-sized, with a fairly long neck, short tail and long **wings**. It has a long, down-curving bill. Ibises eat insects, snails, **carrion** and other animal material. They live in **colonies** of several thousand birds.

ichthyosaur *noun*

Ichthyosaurs were **reptiles** which lived about 200 million years ago. They are now **extinct**. Ichthyosaurs lived in the sea and were between five and thirteen metres long, with a long, sword-like snout. They were carnivores and fed on fish.

iguana *noun*

Iguanas are **reptiles**. Most are found in **deserts** and dry areas in North America and South America. Some live in Madagascar and Fiji. Iguanas are **lizards**. Some species can grow over one and a half metres long. Iguanas feed on flowers, fruits, insects and small invertebrates. They live on the ground or in trees. Female iguanas dig a tunnel in which to lay their eggs.

imago *noun*
An imago is the final stage of
metamorphosis of an **insect**. It is the
perfectly formed adult insect that comes out
of the **pupa**.

immature *adjective*
Immature is used to describe an animal that
is not fully grown or developed. An immature
animal cannot reproduce and is **infertile**.
Newborn animals are also known as
immature. The opposite of immature is
mature.

impala *noun*
An impala is a graceful **mammal**. It is a
species of **antelope**. The impala is found in
large herds on the **savanna** and in the
woodlands of central and southern Africa.
It has a glossy, reddish-brown coat, and a
black stripe on each thigh. Male impalas
have a pair of long horns. Impalas can leap
as far as nine metres and as high as three
metres. Impalas are **herbivores**, and feed
on grass, leaves, flowers and fruit.

incisor ► **tooth**

incubate *verb*
To incubate is to keep **eggs** warm until they
hatch. Animals incubate eggs by using their
body heat. **Birds** incubate their eggs by
sitting on them. Some **reptiles** also incubate
their eggs. Female **pythons** curl their body
around their eggs to keep them warm.

indigenous *adjective*
Indigenous describes an animal or plant that
is only found in a certain area. The **aye-aye**
is indigenous to Madagascar. **Lyrebirds** are
indigenous to Australia. **Piranhas** are
indigenous to South America.

indri *noun*
An indri is a slender **mammal**. It is a
member of the **lemur** family and lives in
trees, only in the **forests** of north-east
Madagascar. Indris are very **rare** and are in
danger of extinction. An indri has long limbs,
a short tail, and a round head with a pointed
face. It is usually black and white. The indri
lives in groups. It is a **herbivore** and feeds
by day on leaves, fruit and shoots.

infertile *adjective*
Infertile describes an animal that cannot
produce young. An animal may be infertile
because it is **immature**. Among **social
insects**, like ants, the workers and soldiers
are infertile all their life. The opposite of
infertile is **fertile**.
infertility *noun*

insect ► page 78

insectivore *noun*
Insectivores are animals that feed mainly on
insects. **Hedgehogs**, **anteaters** and
shrews are examples of insectivores.

insect *noun*

Insects are **invertebrates**. They form part of the group, or **phylum**, called **arthropods**. All insects belong to the same **class**. Scientists have named nearly one million species of insects, including **beetles**, **flies** and **butterflies**. There may be up to 10 million species yet to be discovered. Insects have six legs but many arthropods have eight. Most insects also have wings and **antennae**. The body of an insect changes during its life. This is called **metamorphosis**. Insects live almost everywhere in the world except the oceans. They eat plants, animals and decaying matter.

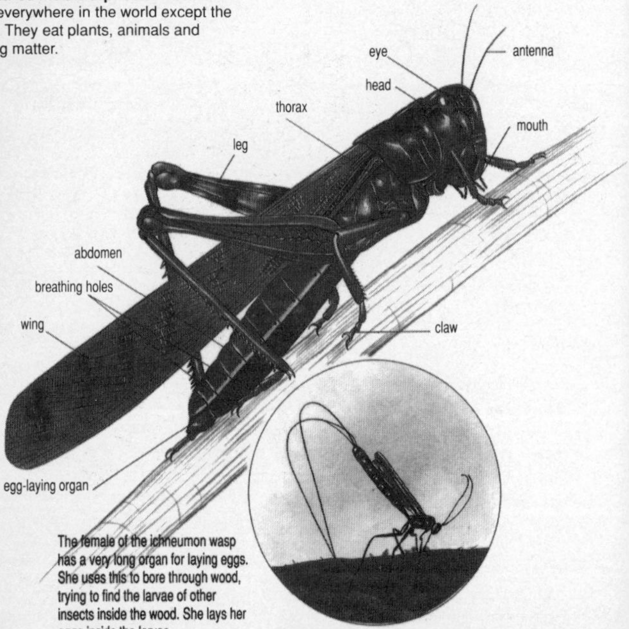

eye

antenna

head

thorax

mouth

leg

abdomen

breathing holes

wing

claw

egg-laying organ

The female of the ichneumon wasp has a very long organ for laying eggs. She uses this to bore through wood, trying to find the larvae of other insects inside the wood. She lays her eggs inside the larvae.

Bees collect a dust called pollen from flowers. As the bee enters the flower to feed on nectar, it catches pollen on its hairy legs. The bee then gathers the pollen into little sacs on its legs.

This moth from Europe has antennae which look like little feathers. They are covered in many hairs. The moth can smell, taste and hear with its antennae.

This mantid has two large compound eyes. Compound eyes are made of hundreds of tiny eyes. They are very sensitive to light and they can see eve small movements. An insect has no eyelids and cannot shut its eyes.

This crane fly from China has very long legs. It can walk very gently because its weight is spread out over a large area.

Beetles have two pairs of wings. The hard wings on the outside protect its body. The wings it uses to fly are inside.

invertebrate   *noun*

An invertebrate is an animal that does not
have a **spine**. **Sponges, jellyfish, worms,
snails** and **spiders** are all invertebrates.
Some invertebrates have a hard **shell** to
protect them. Invertebrates live in all parts of
the world. There are more than one million
known species of invertebrate. They are
sorted into groups of similar animals, each
called a **phylum**. The opposite of
invertebrate is **vertebrate**.

All these are arthropods.

All these are sponges:

All these are worms.

All these are molluscs.

instinct *noun*

Instinct describes the way in which some animals behave naturally. Instinct does not have to be learned. **Birds** fly by instinct. Some **eels** travel long journeys from areas of **fresh water** to the sea, guided by their instinct.

instinctive *adjective*

invertebrate ► page 80

J

jaguar *noun*

Jaguars are powerful **mammals** belonging to the **cat** family. They live in **forests** and **savanna** in Central America and South America. A jaguar has yellow to reddish-brown fur covered with black spots. It usually hunts at night. Jaguars often climb trees and lie in wait for their prey of mammals and birds. They are solitary animals and males and females only live together during the **mating** season.

jellyfish *noun*

Jellyfish are **invertebrates** that are found in all the world's **oceans**. Jellyfish have a soft body shaped like a bell. They do not have any bones. The body is made up of two layers of **cells**, with a jelly-like substance between the layers. Tentacles hang down from the body. Jellyfish feed on plankton and small animals which they catch in their tentacles. Jellyfish reproduce asexually by **budding**.

jerboa   *noun*
Jerboas are small, furry **mammals**. There
are 25 species of jerboa. They live in
deserts and dry areas in Africa, Asia and
eastern Europe. Jerboas have short front
legs, long, powerful back legs and a long
tail. They can take huge leaps, using their
tail to balance. Jerboas are **rodents**. They
live in groups in burrows. At night, they leave
the burrow to find grass, seeds and fruits to
eat. Some species **hibernate** during cold
weather.

joint   *noun*
A joint is the place in the body of a
vertebrate where two bones meet. Most
joints, like those found in the leg, act as a
cushion between bones, allowing them to
move easily. Other joints, like those in the
skull, are fixed and almost rigid.

jungle ► **rain forest**

K

kangaroo   *noun*
Kangaroos are large **mammals**. There are
about 47 species in the kangaroo **family**,
found in **forests** and **grasslands** of
Australia and New Guinea. They are
herbivores. Kangaroos have a small head,
pointed snout, a long tail and large, powerful
back legs. They hop on their back legs,
using their tail for balance, and can reach a
speed of 64 kilometres per hour. They can
leap over one and a half metres high.
Kangaroos are **marsupials** and newborn
kangaroos stay in the mother's pouch for
several months while they grow.

killer whale   *noun*
The killer whale is a large **mammal**. It is the
largest member of the **dolphin** family and is
found in all the **oceans**. Killer whales have a
streamlined body with a black back and
white belly and a triangular dorsal **fin** which
can be almost two metres high. They have a
blunt snout, with between 40 and 50 teeth.
Killer whales can grow as long as nine
metres. They live and hunt in groups, using
echo-location to find food, such as fish,
squid, birds and seals.

kingdom *noun*
A kingdom is part of the system of animal **classification**. A kingdom is the largest group. All animals belong to the animal kingdom. Tiny organisms called protozoa belong to the **protista** kingdom.

kingfisher *noun*
Kingfishers are brightly-coloured **birds**. There are about 85 species of kingfisher living in all parts of the world, usually near inland waters. A kingfisher has a stocky body, short neck and large head. It nests in a tunnel which it digs in the river bank, in a hole in a tree or in a **termite** nest. Some species dive for fish. Others eat insects, small reptiles or even birds and rodents.

kinkajou *noun*
A kinkajou is a small **mammal** that lives in the **rain forests** of Central America and South America. It has light brown fur, a round head and a **prehensile** tail which it uses to grip trees when climbing. Kinkajous are **nocturnal**, and feed at night on insects, small mammals and honey.

kiwi *noun*
Kiwis are brown **birds**. The three species of kiwi live in **forests** in New Zealand. Kiwis have a plump body, short, stocky legs and no tail. They cannot fly. Their bill is long and curved, with nostrils at the end. Kiwis find food by smell. They poke about on the forest floor looking for worms, insects and berries.

klipspringer *noun*
The klipspringer is a hoofed **mammal**. It is a small **antelope**, which is found in the rocky hills of Africa. Klipspringers have a stocky body, short horns and a stumpy tail. Their hooves are rubbery and help them to grip when they are climbing rocks. Klipspringers are herbivores and feed mainly on leaves, flowers and fruit. They live in pairs, or occasionally small herds. They are thought to stay with the same **mate** for life.

koala *noun*
A koala is a furry **mammal**. It is found in **forests** in Australia. Koalas have round ears, a large nose, sharp, curved claws and no tail. They spend all of their time in the trees, only coming to the ground to move to another tree. Koalas are **marsupials**. A young koala spends several months in its mother's pouch and then is carried on her back for about six months. Koalas only feed on the shoots and leaves of eucalyptus trees which also supply their water.

Komodo dragon *noun*
The Komodo dragon is a large **reptile**. It is the largest member of the **lizard** family and grows to about three metres long. It is found in **grasslands** on the island of Komodo and on nearby islands in Indonesia. The Komodo dragon has a thick body and long tail. It has strong claws and large teeth. Although big, the Komodo dragon is a good climber and can move quickly. It lives in **burrows**. The Komodo dragon is a **carnivore**. Its diet includes deer, wild boar and pigs.

kookaburra *noun*
The kookaburra is a **bird**. It is a member of the **kingfisher** family and lives in woods in Australia. The kookaburra has a grey back and **wings**, and a white head and underparts. It is the largest of the kingfishers, at 46 centimetres long. It is known as the laughing kookaburra because the sound it makes is like laughter. The kookaburra eats insects and small reptiles.

83

krill   *noun*
Krill are small **invertebrates**. There are
over 90 species of krill, found in **oceans**
throughout the world. Krill are **crustaceans**
and look like **shrimps**. They live in large
groups called swarms. Krill use organs that
give off bright light by **bioluminescence** to
search for food and to attract a mate. They
are an important source of food for many
species of fish, birds and whales.

kudu   *noun*
Kudus are slender **mammals**. There are two
species of kudu, found in **grasslands** in
southern and eastern Africa. They are large
antelopes. Kudus have a pair of horns and
hoofed feet. They live in small herds. Kudus
are **herbivores** and feed on grass, seeds
and shoots.

L

lamprey   *noun*
Lampreys are long, slender **fish**. Some
species of lamprey live in the North Atlantic
and North Pacific oceans. Others are found
in rivers and lakes in Europe, Asia and North
America. Lampreys do not have any bones,
scales or jaws and the skeleton is made of
cartilage. They have a round mouth with
small, horny teeth. Many species of lamprey
are **parasites**. They attach themselves to
fish with their teeth and then suck their
blood. Lampreys are similar to **hagfish**.

lantern fish   *noun*
Lantern fish are small **fish**. There are more
than 230 species of them living in large
groups, called schools, deep in the sea.
Lantern fish use organs that give off light by
bioluminescence to attract prey and to
communicate with each other. These organs
are found on the head, the sides of the body
and the tail. Lantern fish feed on **plankton**.
They spend the day deep in the ocean, but
rise nearer to the surface at night.

lark   *noun*
Larks are small, dull-coloured **birds**. There
are about 75 species of lark which live in
open **habitats**, such as **desert**, **tundra** and
grassland. They are found in Europe, Asia
and Africa. Larks have long wings and a bill
that curves downwards. They spend most of
their time and also nest on the ground. Larks
eat seeds, buds and insects. They use
birdsong in **courtship**. They fly high into
the sky, singing their clear, loud song as they
go. Female larks lay three to five eggs in a
grass nest.

larva (plural **larvae**) *noun*
A larva is an immature stage in the **life cycle** of some animals. In the **metamorphosis** of insects, the larva is the soft grub that hatches out of the egg. An **amphibian** also has a larva. A tadpole is the larva of a frog.

lateral line system *noun*
The lateral line system is the row of sensitive areas which lie along the head and sides of **fish** and some **amphibians**. These areas can feel any movement of water or any change in the force of the water.

leech *noun*
Leeches are **invertebrates**. They are found in **fresh water** and on damp ground. Leeches are **worms** and have a body made up of segments with a sucker at each end. The small sucker at the front contains the mouth and teeth. Some species of leech eat plants or decaying animal material. Others are **parasites** and feed on the blood of animals. They attach themselves to the skin of the animal with their suckers, bite into the flesh and then suck out the blood.

lemming *noun*
Lemmings are small, furry **mammals**. They are found in the northern areas of Europe, Asia and North America. They are **rodents**. Lemmings usually live in groups in **burrows**. They are **herbivores** and feed on plants and roots.

lemur *noun*
Lemurs are furry **mammals**. The **indri** and the **aye-aye** are species of lemur. Lemurs are **primates** which can only be found in the wooded areas of Madagascar and the islands nearby. Lemurs have a long, bushy tail and long back legs. They range in size from the tiny mouse lemurs to the large indris, which are about 75 centimetres long. They are agile and spend most of their time in trees. Lemurs are **omnivores**. Their diet includes fruit, leaves, insects, birds and birds' eggs. Some species of lemur are **rare** and threatened with extinction.

leopard *noun*
Leopards are large **mammals**. They are members of the **cat** family. They live alone in the **plains** and **forests** of Africa and Asia. Leopards have a light-coloured coat covered with dark spots. They are **carnivores** and feed on such animals as antelope, deer, snakes and goats. Leopards are agile and climb trees well. They sometimes store their prey up in the trees.

life cycle *noun*
A life cycle describes the series of changes that take place in an animal as it grows into an adult. The life cycle lasts from the time the animal is a **fertilized** egg until it is a **fertile** adult, producing young of its own. **Amphibians** have three stages in their life cycle. These are egg, tadpole and adult. Insects go through three or four different stages called **metamorphosis**. The life cycle of **mammals** goes from egg, to embryo, to young, to adult.

limpet *noun*
Limpets are **invertebrates**. They are small **molluscs** and are found on rocks in **oceans** throughout the world. They live near the coast. Limpets have a soft body covered with a cone-shaped shell and a long tongue with rows of teeth on it. They have a muscular foot which they use to cling to rocks where they browse on algae.

85

linsang *noun*
Linsangs are small, slender **mammals**. The
two species are members of the **civet** family.
Linsangs live in **forests**. One species is
found in Africa and the other in South-east
Asia. Linsangs have a long body and
yellowish-grey fur with dark spots or bands.
They have a long, dark-ringed tail. Linsangs
are **nocturnal** and hunt at night for birds,
insects, and small mammals and reptiles.

lion *noun*
Lions are large **mammals**. They belong to
the **cat** family. They live on grassy **plains**
and open **savanna** in southern Africa and
north- west India. A lion has a long body,
short legs and a large head. Male lions have
a thick mane of hair, that covers their head,
neck and shoulders. They are **carnivores**
and feed on large **prey**, such as zebra and
buffalo. The female lion, called a lioness,
usually does the hunting.

lizard *noun*
Lizards are **reptiles**. There are over 3,000
species including the **gecko**, **iguana** and
komodo dragon. They live mainly in the
tropics and are found in dry areas, such as
deserts. Lizards have a dry, scaly skin, a
long tail and clawed toes. Lizards are **cold-
blooded** animals and vary in size, shape
and colour. They feed on insects, small
animals and plants. Most lizards lay eggs
but some give birth to live young.

loach *noun*
Loach are small freshwater **fish**. Most are
found in Asia, but a few species live in
Europe and one in Africa. Loach have a long
body, very small scales and whiskers, or
barbels, around their mouth. They feed on
the bottom, eating small water animals such
as worms and insect larvae.

lobster *noun*
Lobsters are **invertebrates**. They live at the
bottom of the Atlantic and Pacific oceans.
They are **crustaceans**. Lobsters have a
segmented body covered with a dark blue or
green shell. They have five pairs of legs,
with two large claws at the end of the front
pair. Their eyes are placed at the end of
stalks. Lobsters live in **burrows** and are
active at night, coming out to catch crabs,
snails and small fish. As lobsters grow, they
moult their shell.

locomotion *noun*
Locomotion is the act of moving around.
Flying and swimming are two kinds of
locomotion.

locust *noun*
Locusts are **insects**. They **migrate** across
every continent except Antarctica. Locusts
have a large head, compound eyes and
short **antennae**. They are a species of
grasshopper. There may be millions of
locusts in a swarm. They feed on vegetation
and destroy crops. Male locusts attract a
mate by rubbing their back legs on their front
wings to make a clicking noise.

loris *noun*
Lorises are furry **mammals** found in Africa and Asia. They make up a family in the **primate** order. A loris has large eyes and either no tail or a short one. They are slow-moving animals and are **nocturnal**. During the day they sleep in the trees, rolled up into a ball with their head tucked between their legs. Lorises are **omnivores** and feed on insects, fruit, leaves and young birds.

lory (plural **lories**) *noun*
Lories are noisy, colourful **birds**, belonging to the **parrot** family. They live in **forests** in southern Asia and Australia. Lories have a short, hooked bill and a long tongue with tufts on the end. They use their special tongue to feed on nectar and pollen from trees and plants. They also eat seeds and fruit. Most species travel great distances in search of food.

lung *noun*
The lung is part of the body of **vertebrates** which live on land. It is used for breathing. There are two lungs, found in the chest. An animal breathes air into the lungs. Oxygen from the air passes into the **blood** and travels around the body. A waste gas called carbon dioxide passes out of the blood, into the lungs and the animal breathes it out.

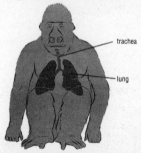
trachea

lung

lungfish *noun*
Lungfish are long, slender **fish**. There are six species of lungfish living in **freshwater** marshes, swamps and rivers in Africa, Australia and South America. Lungfish can breathe in two ways. They can breathe under water, using their **gills**. They can also breathe out of water with their **swim bladder**. Lungfish feed on small fish, frogs and snails.

lynx *noun*
Lynxes are **mammals**. They belong to the **cat** family and are found in the **forests** of Africa, Asia, Europe and North America. The African lynx is called the **caracal**. Lynxes have a short tail and tufts of hair on their ears and cheeks. They are good climbers and like to lie stretched out on the branch of a tree. They usually live alone. Lynxes hunt at night, and their **prey** includes hares, rodents and birds.

lyrebird *noun*
Lyrebirds are brown-coloured **birds**. There are two species of lyrebird, only found in the **forests** of Australia. Males have long, bushy tail feathers that they raise during **courtship**. They often spread their tail over their head. Lyrebirds mainly live on the ground, and rarely fly. They build large nests of grass, plants and twigs in which the female lays one egg. Lyrebirds have a loud song, and they can also **mimic** the songs of other birds. Lyrebirds feed on insects and larva.

M

macaque   *noun*
Macaques are **monkeys**. There are
15 different species of macaque. Most live in
Asia, but one species lives in North Africa..
Macaques have large jaws and strong,
sharp teeth with which they eat fruit, insects,
fish, birds, small mammals and even crabs.
They can run and climb well.

mackerel   *noun*
Mackerel are **fish**. They are found in coastal
areas of the Atlantic, Pacific and Indian
oceans. They live in large shoals near the
surface of the sea. Mackerel have strong
muscles and can swim very fast. They feed
on crustaceans and small fish.

male   *adjective*
Male describes those animals which
produce male sex cells, or **sperm**. The
opposite of male is **female**. Male animals
pass their sperm to the female during
mating. In many animals, such as **birds**, the
male is more brightly coloured than the
female. Some male **mammals** have the
same mate for life. Others have several
different mates at the same time.

mamba   *noun*
Mambas are poisonous **snakes** found in
Africa. They can climb well and feed on birds
and small mammals. Mambas belong to the
same family as **cobras**. Snakes in this
family all have short, rigid fangs at the front
of their mouth, and are also known as front-
fanged snakes.

mammal ► page 90

mammary gland   *noun*
Mammary glands are special **glands** found
on the chest of mammals. When a female
mammal has a baby, these glands swell up
with **milk**. The baby sucks the milk from its
mother's mammary glands. **Primates** have
two mammary glands, but many mammals
have several, arranged in two rows.

mammoth   *noun*
Mammoths were large **mammals** which
lived many thousands of years ago. They
are now **extinct**. Like **elephants**, they had
long tusks and trunks, but their hair was
much thicker, and reddish in colour. They
are sometimes found frozen in ice.

manatee   *noun*
Manatees are large **mammals.** The three
species are found in warm, clear waters of
southern North America, South America and
West Africa. Manatees spend all their life in
the water, swimming slowly and grazing on
the bottom of the sea or river. Like their
relatives the **dugongs**, manatees are
herbivores and feed on waterweeds.

mandrill   *noun*
A mandrill is a kind of **monkey**, belonging to
the **baboon** family. The male mandrill is
about 80 centimetres long and is much
larger than the female. The mandrill has a
colourful face, with a red nose and patches
of bright blue skin. Mandrills live in the **rain
forests** of western Central Africa. They eat
fruit, seeds, roots, insects and other small
animals.

mantid *noun*
A mantid, or mantis, is a large **insect**. There are about 1,800 species, mainly found in **tropical** countries. Mantids move slowly in trees and grass. They have large front legs and sharp claws with which they catch smaller insects to eat. A mantid is sometimes called a praying mantis because it holds its front legs together, as if in prayer.

marine *adjective*
Marine describes an animal which lives in the sea. Marine mammals include **whales** and **dolphins**, and most **snails** are also marine. Marine animals are usually able to swim or float in the water.

marlin *noun*
Marlins are large marine **fish**. There are 10 species of marlin, and they belong to the same family as sailfish. Marlins swim very fast, and have been timed at a speed of up to 80 kilometres per hour. They live in the warm waters near the surface of the sea, and feed on smaller fish. Marlins are very streamlined, with a pointed snout and large dorsal fin.

marmoset *noun*
Marmosets are small **monkeys** which live in the **rain forests** of South America. The seven species of marmoset are slightly smaller than their relatives, the **tamarins**. They live in small groups among the trees. They have delicate hands and a long, furry tail. Marmosets use their sharp teeth to bite holes in tree bark and then lick up the sweet gum which oozes out.

marmot *noun*
Marmots are plump **rodents** which live in **mountain** areas of Europe, Asia and North America. There are 15 species of marmot. They are the largest members of the **squirrel** family. The woodchuck of North America is a kind of marmot. Marmots dig underground **burrows**, in which they hibernate during the cold winter weather.

marsh habitat *noun*
Marsh habitats are those areas of land in which the water level is very high. The ground in a marsh is nearly always soggy and not firm to walk on. Plants such as some mosses, sedges and rushes grow in marshes. Animals of marsh habitats include frogs, wading birds, ducks and otters.

marsupial ► page 92

marten *noun*
Martens are long, slender **mammals**. There are eight species of marten which belong to the **weasel** family. Most martens live in coniferous woodland, and they are expert climbers. They feed on birds, eggs and smaller mammals, and can even chase and catch squirrels. Martens have soft, thick fur which keeps them warm in cold weather.

mastodon *noun*
Mastodons are **extinct** animals which were a little like **elephants**. Some kinds of mastodon lived until about 10,000 years ago. Mastodons had shorter and heavier bodies than elephants and they had tusks in their upper and lower jaws.

mate *verb*
Mate describes the process by which the male animal passes **sperm** to the female animal, in **sexual reproduction**. Mating animals bring their bodies close together, so that the sperm from the male can reach the **eggs** of the female.

mammal *noun*

A mammal is a **vertebrate** which is hairy and has four legs or limbs. Mammals are a **class** of animal and scientists have named more than 4,000 **species**. Female mammals give birth to live young and feed them on milk from their breasts, or **mammary glands**. Most mammals have a large brain. Mammals are **warm-blooded**, so they stay the same temperature no matter how hot or cold it is. This means that some mammals, such as **polar bears**, can live at the North Pole and others, such as **camels**, can live in deserts. Most mammals live on the land, but **whales** and **dolphins** live in the oceans and **bats** can fly.

Female mammals, such as chimpanzees, are ready to mate at particular times of the year. Many female mammals may show the male they are ready to mate by changing colour or by producing a special smell.

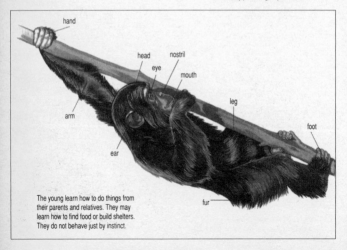

hand

head   nostril

eye   mouth

leg

arm

foot

ear

fur

The young learn how to do things from their parents and relatives. They may learn how to find food or build shelters. They do not behave just by instinct.

Mammals reproduce by sexual reproduction. The male chimpanzee fertilizes the egg inside the female's body. In all mammals except the marsupials and the monotremes, the young animal grows inside the mother's body.

When the young chimpanzee is born, the mother cares for it. All female mammals feed their young with milk that they make inside their body.

The young do not leave their mother until they are fully grown and can bring up a family of their own. This is a young, fully-grown chimpanzee.

marsupial *noun*

A marsupial is a **mammal** that usually has a pouch. A baby marsupial is born after a very short time, or **gestation**, inside its mother's body. The young are very small and not fully developed. They complete their development attached to their mother's teat. **Kangaroos**, **koalas** and **opossums** are all marsupials. Marsupials are found only in Australia, North and South America. They live in **forests**, **plains** and **deserts**.

Young opossums begin their life inside their mother's body. They are born only 12 days after the eggs were fertilized. Their ears, eyes and back legs have not grown. They crawl up the mother's body to the pouch on her abdomen. Here, they feed on milk from her mammary glands.

The baby kangaroo leaves its mother's pouch after about six months. But it still comes back to feed on her milk and jumps inside if there is any danger.

The baby koala grows inside its mother's pouch until it is about six months old. Then it leaves the pouch, and spends the next few months riding around on its mother's back.

mate *noun*
A mate is the partner that an animal chooses for **sexual reproduction**. Some animals choose one mate for life, others may have more than one mate. Many animals share the task of looking after eggs and young with their mate.

mature *adjective*
Mature describes an animal which has grown to become an adult. As animals grow from the young stage, they gradually gain adult **characteristics**. They become more and more mature. Mature animals are able to breed and have young of their own.

mayfly *noun*
Mayflies are delicate **insects**. They live for only a short time as adults, often for less than a day. There are about 2,000 species of mayfly. Adult mayflies have clear, triangular front wings and fly over rivers, streams and ponds. The young of mayflies, called **nymphs**, live under the water, sometimes inside tubes made of stones or leaves.

medusa ► jellyfish

meerkat *noun*
A meerkat is a small, active **mammal**. It belongs to the **mongoose** family and there is only one species. Meerkats are found in dry areas of southern Africa. They live in groups in underground **burrows**, which they dig in the dry soil. They often stand upright on their mound, watching for any sign of danger.

megapode *noun*
Megapodes are large **birds**. There are 12 species of megapode, which live in Australia, New Guinea and South-east Asia. They are brown, grey and black in colour. Megapodes live in **forests**, woodland and scrub and they eat fruits, seeds, and insects. The most famous megapode is the mallee fowl, which lays its eggs under a large mound of leaves and soil.

membrane *noun*
A membrane is a thin layer of **cells** inside an animal's body. It is made of a substance called connective tissue. Membranes surround or separate **organs** such as the **heart**. They also line hollows, or cavities inside the body, such as the **abdomen**.

metamorphosis ► page 94

migration ► page 96

milk *noun*
Milk is a white liquid. It is produced in the **mammary glands** of female **mammals** when they have young. Baby mammals drink milk as their first food. Milk is very nourishing. It contains large amounts of substances needed for **growth**, such as protein and calcium.

millipede *noun*
Millipedes are shiny **arthropods** which have many pairs of legs. There are about 10,000 species of millipede, mostly found in **tropical** countries. A millipede's body is divided into segments, and each segment has two pairs of legs. Some millipedes have as many as 240 pairs of legs. Most have fewer than 100 pairs. Millipedes eat plants and dead leaves.

mimicry *noun*
Mimicry describes what happens when an animal of one species looks like or copies the behaviour of an animal of another species. Many animals mimic poisonous species to avoid being eaten. A **bird** which recognizes and avoids eating a poisonous **butterfly** will also avoid eating a non-poisonous butterfly which mimics the poisonous one. Birds use mimicry when they copy the songs of other species.
mimic *verb*

metamorphosis   *noun*

Metamorphosis is a major change in the shape or form of an animal's body. It takes place in some animals as they grow into adults. Metamorphosis takes place in **insects**, **amphibians** and some sea animals. Many insects, such as butterflies, beetles, flies and wasps, pass through a complete metamorphosis. The four stages are **egg**, **larva**, **pupa** and adult. Other insects, such as grasshoppers and cockroaches, pass through only three stages, of egg, larva and adult. The larva looks like the adult insect.

Complete metamorphosis of a butterfly

The butterfly has laid an egg on a leaf. Inside the egg, the embryo is forming. The larva will eat the leaf when it hatches.

The larva hatches out of the egg. It is a soft grub with no wings and doesn't look like an adult butterfly. The larva eats plants. It can eat and grow but it cannot reproduce. The larva grows rapidly and moults or sheds its skin many times. The larvae of butterflies and moths are also called caterpillars.

The larva has become a pupa. Inside this chrysalis, all the body parts of the larva are broken down into a liquid and rebuilt as the adult butterfly.

The adult insect, called the imago, has broken open the shell of the pupa and is pulling itself out.

After waiting a few minutes for the blood to reach its wings, the butterfly is strong enough to fly away.

Incomplete metamorphosis of a dragonfly

nymph

nymph changes into dragonfly

adult dragonfly

migration *noun*

Migration is the movement of animals to a place where it is easier for them to live. Animals such as the **plover** migrate at particular times of the year to a warmer place or to an area where there is more food. Some animals, such as the **eel** and the **turtle**, migrate to a particular region to lay their eggs. Most biologists use the word migration to describe regular journeys, where the animal travels to the new place and back again.

migrate *verb*

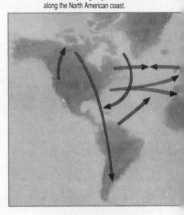

Caribou live in North America. They travel north, into the Arctic tundra, during the warm season. They return south to breed when the cold season comes.

Fur seals breed in the far north of the Pacific Ocean. In the cold season, they migrate south in small groups. The females and young may swim far south along the North American coast.

Golden plovers breed in Alaska. In the cold season, they migrate to South America. Some birds even fly to Hawaii. The birds follow a different route to travel back to Alaska.

Green turtles live in the shallow waters on the east coast of South America. To breed, they swim east to a tiny island in the middle of the southern Atlantic.

96

Salmon are born in freshwater rivers in Europe and North America. After several years, they move into the sea and grow there for several years. Then the fish return to the same stream that they were born in to spawn.

The European eel is born in an area of water near Central America called the Sargasso Sea. The young eels take three years to travel across the Atlantic Ocean. When they reach Europe, they live in freshwater rivers. After several years, they return to the Sargasso Sea to breed.

Bewick's swan breeds in the tundra of northern Russia and Siberia. In the cold season, it migrates south to Europe.

The short-tailed shearwater lives and breeds in the seas south of Australia. It migrates in a huge figure-of-eight travelling right up to the north of the Pacific Ocean.

mink *noun*

Mink are slender **mammals** which belong to the weasel family. There are two species of mink, one found in North America and the other in Europe. Mink live near rivers and lakes. They have thick, sleek fur and a long tail. Mink are **carnivores** and hunt for water birds, small mammals and fish. The American species is bred on farms for its fur which is made into expensive coats.

mite *noun*

Mites are tiny **arthropods**. Mites and **ticks** make up the same order and there are about 30,000 species altogether. Mites have very small bodies, often smaller than a pin-head, and eight legs. Some mites eat plants and fungi, and others are **carnivorous**. Some live as **parasites** on the bodies of other animals.

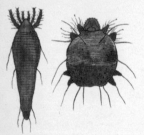

mockingbird *noun*

Mockingbirds are medium-sized **birds**. There are 30 different species, all found in North and South America. They are brown-coloured, with a long, flared tail. Mockingbirds take their name from the way some species **mimic** other songs and sounds, including the human voice. They eat insects, seeds and fruits. Mockingbirds nest in trees and bushes, and lay from four to six **eggs**.

molar ► tooth

mole *noun*

Moles are small **mammals**. There are 29 species of mole, and they are found in North America, Europe and Asia. Moles are **insectivores** which live underground. They burrow in the soil, using their spade-like front feet. Moles have tiny eyes and can see only very poorly. They spend most of their life in the darkness of their **burrow**, where they feed on earthworms, beetles and slugs.

mollusc *noun*

Molluscs are soft-bodied **invertebrates** with hard shells. There are about 100,000 species and three main **classes** of mollusc. These are **snails** and their relatives, **bivalves**, **octopuses** and **squids**. Most molluscs have a file-like tongue which they use to scrape up their food.

mongoose *noun*

Mongooses are **mammals**. There are about 31 species, in the same family as **civets** and **genets**. Most mongooses live in Africa and Asia. They have a long, slender body. Mongooses live in forests and open woodland. They are **carnivores** and eat insects and small vertebrates, including snakes.

monitor lizard *noun*

Monitor lizards are the largest of all **lizards**. There are about 30 species, found in Africa, Asia and Australia. They are **carnivores**, feeding on smaller animals which they kill with their powerful jaws. The most famous monitor is the **Komodo dragon**.

monkey *noun*

Monkeys are active **mammals**. There are about 130 species of monkey, including howler monkeys, marmosets, tamarins and baboons. They belong to the order of **primates**, which also includes **apes** and humans. Monkeys live in the forests of Africa, South-east Asia and South America, and most species climb very well. They have well-developed hands, eyes and brains. Monkeys are **omnivores**.

monocular vision ► eye

monotreme *adjective*
Monotreme describes an unusual kind of **mammal** which lays eggs and has no teeth. There are only three species of monotreme mammals. These are the two kinds of **spiny anteater**, or echidna, and the **platypus**. Spiny anteaters live in Australia and New Guinea, and the platypus only in eastern Australia. Monotreme young feed on their mother's milk after hatching from the eggs.

moose *noun*
A moose is a large **mammal**. It is the largest member of the **deer** family. Moose live in northern Europe, Asia and North America. They have also been introduced to New Zealand. The male moose has large, spreading antlers. It can grow to be 230 centimetres tall at the shoulder. Moose usually live alone. They are **herbivores**, and eat woody plants and some water plants.

mosquito *noun*
Mosquitoes are **insects**, with sharp, piercing mouthparts. Female mosquitoes use these to suck blood from the skin of mammals. There are about 3,000 species of mosquito. They lay their eggs on the surface of a pond or puddle. The **larvae** hatch out and live under the water before changing into adults and flying off. Some mosquitoes carry diseases, such as malaria.

moth *noun*
Moths are flying **insects**. There are more than 100,000 species of moth, in the same **order** as **butterflies**. Moths have large wings covered in scales. They often have feathery feelers, or **antennae**, and duller colours than butterflies. Most moths fly at dusk or in the night.

moult *verb*
Moult is the word used to describe the process of shedding **skin**. Many animals increase in size by losing a top layer of skin and growing a new, stretchy layer underneath. When the old skin is moulted, the body grows as the new skin expands.

mountain habitat *noun*
Mountain habitats are areas found high up in mountain regions. They include alpine **grassland**, rocky slopes, fast-flowing rivers and snow patches. Mountain habitats become very cold in winter and at night. They are also very windy. **Mammals** of mountain habitats need thick fur and often **hibernate** in the winter.

mouse (plural **mice**) *noun*
Mice are small **mammals**. There are over 1,000 species in the mouse family, which includes **rats**. Mice are **rodents** and are found all over the world. They are very active and have round, black eyes, soft fur and a long tail. They eat mostly grain, fruit and insects.

mouth *noun*

The mouth is an opening in the head of an animal. It is the part of the body where an animal takes in food. Many animals have **teeth** inside their mouth, to bite and grind food. The teeth sit in a bony structure which moves, called the jaw. Other animals have a **bill** or bony plates instead of teeth. Some **insects** do not have jaws or teeth. They have mouthparts which are adapted to sucking liquid food.

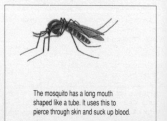

A chimpanzee has lips around its mouth. It moves these into different expressions. This chimpanzee is saying hello.

A snake has special jaws which are not joined to each other and it can open its mouth very wide. It swallows its prey whole and does not chew it. Some snakes can even swallow an animal as large as an antelope.

A shark's mouth is full of sharp teeth, in as many as 20 rows. As the front row wears down, the rows behind push forward and replace the front teeth.

This beetle has strong jaws which chew and grind up its food. The jaws move from side to side.

The mosquito has a long mouth shaped like a tube. It uses this to pierce through skin and suck up blood.

mousedeer *noun*
Mousedeer are tiny, hoofed **mammals**. There are four species, which live in the **tropical rain forests** of Africa, India and South-east Asia. The smallest measures less than 50 centimetres from head to tail. Mousedeer have no antlers, but the males have a pair of long, sharp teeth in the upper jaw. Mousedeer eat fruit and leaves.

mouth ► page 100

mucus *noun*
Mucus is a slimy substance which is made by special **cells** in an animal's body. It is found in the **mouth**, where it helps to trap particles of food during feeding. Mucus also traps grit and dust in the nose and throat. It prevents these entering the lungs during **breathing**.

mudpuppy *noun*
Mudpuppies are **salamanders**. There are five species found in freshwater streams in North America. Some mudpuppies grow as long as 40 centimetres. The olm of Europe belongs to the same family, but is much smaller. Mudpuppies lay their eggs under stones in sunny streams where they hatch into small **larvae**.

mudskipper *noun*
Mudskippers are small **fish** which can breathe air. They live in muddy estuaries in Africa, South-east Asia and Australia. They spend much of their time out of the water and move by balancing on their front fins and wriggling and jumping. They are common in mangrove swamps and can even climb up tree roots and branches.

muscle *noun*
Muscles are special groups of **cells** in an animal's body, which move together. All animals use muscles when they move. Muscles are attached to bones by tendons, and they pull against the bones to make parts of an animal move.

musk deer *noun*
Musk deer are small, shy **mammals**. There are three species of musk deer, which live in mountain forests in eastern Asia. They are about one metre long from head to tail, and have no antlers. Male musk deer have sharp, pointed teeth which stick out over their lower lip, like tusks. Musk deer mark their territories with a special, strong-smelling substance called musk.

musk ox *noun*
A musk ox is a large **mammal**. It is in the same family as **goats**, **antelope** and **bison**. It is found on the **tundra** of Alaska and Greenland. The musk ox is protected against the extreme cold by its long, thick coat. Its hooves are very broad, so it does not sink into the snow. Musk oxen feed mainly on grass and other plants. They live in large groups of up to 100.

muskrat *noun*
A muskrat is a large rodent. It belongs to the same family as **voles** and is found in North America. Muskrats have also been introduced to Europe and Asia. They spend most of their time in water. Muskrats live in nests, called houses, made of branches and twigs in marshes and riverbanks. They are excellent swimmers, using their flat, scaly tail as a rudder. Muskrats eat mainly plants, and sometimes small water animals. They produce litters of up to 11 young, two to three times a year.

mussel *noun*
Mussels are **molluscs**. They are **bivalves**, which means they have two shells. The shells are hinged together and enclose a soft, flattened body. Mussels are found throughout the world. Most live in the sea, but a few live in fresh water. A mussel attaches itself firmly to a shell or a rock by threads from its narrow foot. It feeds by filtering out tiny plant and animal cells from the water.

mutation *noun*
Mutation is the way the **genes** of animals change, and give the animals different **characteristics**. Many mutations happen naturally. But they can also be caused by chemicals or by radiation. A mutation may be harmful, or it may give the animal some advantage. An animal with a mutated gene may look or behave differently from its parents. **Albino** animals have white fur because their body carries a mutation of the gene which gives hair colour.

myna *noun*
Mynas are tropical **birds**, related to **starlings**. There are about 12 species of myna, all found in Asia. They have glossy plumage, and a narrow, sharp bill. Mynas live in groups in trees. They feed on fruit, buds and nectar. They also eat insects and lizards. The female myna lays two or three eggs in a nest inside a tree trunk. Both parents look after the eggs and the young. Mynas can **mimic** many different sounds, including the human voice.

N

narwhal *noun*
A narwhal is a marine **mammal**. It belongs to the white **whale** family, together with the **beluga**. Narwhals live in the Arctic Ocean. They are a mottled colour, grey-green with blotches of cream and black. Narwhals grow four to five metres long. The male narwhal has a spiral, ivory tusk, which can be nearly three metres long. The tusk is one of the narwhal's two teeth. Narwhals live in groups of six to ten. They feed on squid, shrimps and fish.

nautilus *noun*
Nautiluses are **molluscs**, related to **octopuses**. Only about six species are known and they are found in the Indian and Pacific oceans. Nautiluses have a heavy, coiled shell. As the animals grow, they seal off old chambers and only live in the new, outermost part. There are gases and liquids in the inner chambers. These help nautiluses to live as deep as 500 metres. Nautiluses have about 90 short, sticky tentacles. They feed on fish.

navigation *noun*
Navigation describes the way animals direct themselves when they move over long distances. During **migration**, animals use navigation to find their way. They may navigate by following the changing shape of the land below them. They may use the patterns of the stars at night, and the angle of the Sun by day. Many birds, and perhaps some mammals, can also navigate by sensing the direction of the Earth's magnetic field.

nerve *noun*
Nerves are long fibres in an animal's body. Nerve fibres are made up of special **cells**, that are covered with a layer of fat. Nerves carry messages through the animal's body. All the nerves link to the spinal cord. They then go to the brain, which is itself a mass of nerve cells. Nerves control an animal's senses, so that it can react to changes in its **environment**. Nerves also enable the different parts of an animal's body to function.

nest *noun*
A nest is a structure which is used by some kinds of animal. Animals build nests to live in and to raise their young. **Social insects**, such as some species of **wasp** and **ant**, make large nests. Most **birds** build nests for laying their eggs and rearing their young. Some birds' nests are simple hollows in the ground. Others are complicated structures woven from materials such as sticks, moss, leaves and feathers. Many **mammals** dig their nests underground, and reach them through tunnels.

newt *noun*
Newts are **amphibians**. They belong to the same family as **salamanders**. Most species of newt live in the tropics and the temperate regions of north-west Africa, Europe, Asia and North America. Unlike salamanders, newts have a flattened tail, with a thin fringe. This helps them to swim. On land, newts move slowly on all fours, or more quickly by wriggling as they do in water. Newts return to fresh water to lay their eggs. The eggs hatch into tadpoles.

nightjar *noun*
Nightjars are **nocturnal birds**. There are 72 species, which are found in most parts of the world. Nightjars have grey, black and brown plumage that looks like bark. They have long, pointed wings and large eyes. Nightjars fly silently at night and catch insects by darting at them. Their mouth can open very wide to catch large insects. Nightjars have weak legs and do not walk well. They roost during the day, when they are well **camouflaged** amongst the trees.

nocturnal *adjective*
Nocturnal describes an animal which is active at night. Many **mammals**, such as the **potto**, are nocturnal. Some birds, such as **owls** and **nightjars**, are nocturnal. There are also millions of nocturnal **insects**, particularly in the tropics. Most nocturnal animals can see and hear very well. They often make loud calls so that they can keep in contact even when out of sight of each other. The opposite of nocturnal is **diurnal**.

nose *noun*
A nose is the part of an animal's body that is used for smelling. The outer nose is made of **cartilage**, covered with skin. Holes inside the outer nose lead to the inner nose. When an animal breathes, chemicals in the air cause **nerves** in the inner nose to react. Nerve messages then pass to the brain and the animal recognizes these as a smell. As the air passes through the nose on its way to the lungs, it is warmed, moistened and dust is filtered out of it.

nuthatch   *noun*
Nuthatches are climbing **birds**. There are
about 20 species of nuthatch, which are
found in North America, Europe, Asia and
Australia. Nuthatches live in woods and
parks where there are old trees. They nest in
holes in trees and cement up the entrance to
their nest with earth and mud. Nuthatches
can climb well, downwards as well as
upwards. They use their pointed bill to probe
cracks in the bark for the insects which are
their main food.

nymph   *noun*
Nymphs are the young, or **immature**, stages
of some land insects. In the process called
metamorphosis, nymphs become adults
without going through a **pupa** stage.
Nymphs look like the adult in some ways,
but lack an adult feature, such as wings.
They cannot reproduce. A newly-hatched
nymph has a pale, delicate skin, and it
moults as it grows. Examples of insects with
nymphs are grasshoppers, cockroaches and
dragonflies.

ocean habitat   *noun*
Oceans cover more than 70 per cent of the
Earth's surface. They are a very important
habitat for living things. There is life in all
parts of the ocean, even where it is at its
deepest. The ocean makes up over 99 per
cent of the inhabited space on the planet.
A wide range of animals lives in the oceans,
from tiny **plankton** to huge **whales**.

ocelot   *noun*
An ocelot is a **mammal**. It is a medium-sized
member of the **cat** family. Ocelots are found
in forests and thick bush country in southern
parts of North America and in South
America. Ocelots have a coat with dark
spots or stripes, and a ringed tail. They are
nocturnal and hunt mammals, birds and
snakes. Ocelots can climb and swim well,
and make safe dens in hollow trees to raise
their young.

octopus   *noun*
Octopuses are **molluscs**. There are about
50 species of octopus. They are found in
tropical and temperate seas throughout the
world. An octopus has eight long arms, or
tentacles. Each tentacle has two rows of
suckers. The octopus uses these for holding
onto rocks, and for catching its prey. Its
mouth has a strong beak. It eats mainly
crabs and other crustaceans. Octopuses are
the most intelligent **invertebrates**. They
learn very quickly and remember simple
tasks for several weeks.

offspring   *noun*
Offspring are the young of an animal.

okapi *noun*
An okapi is a rare **mammal**. It belongs to the **giraffe** family, but has a much shorter neck than giraffes. Okapis live in the **rain forests** around the Congo River, in Africa. They have a brown body, and white stripes on their legs. Okapis have a long, black tongue, which they use to feed on the leaves or young shoots of forest trees. They have poor eyesight, but they have a strong sense of smell and hearing. The okapi was not discovered until 1900, and little is known about its **behaviour**.

omnivore *noun*
An omnivore is an animal that eats a varied diet of animal and plant material. **Chimpanzees** are òmnivores. With their three kinds of **teeth** – incisors, canines and molars – they can eat the meat of other animals as well as insects, leaves, fruit and nuts.

chimpanzee skull

opossum *noun*
Opossums are **marsupial mammals**. There are about 75 species of opossum, mostly found in South America and Central America. One species also lives in North America. Opossums are shaped like rats, with a scaly tail and untidy fur. They are solitary animals and most live in **forests**. Opossums are **nocturnal**. They eat most kinds of animal or plant food. Like other marsupials, baby opossums live first of all in their mother's pouch.

orang-utan *noun*
An orang-utan is a large **primate**. It is the second largest **ape**, after the **gorilla**. Orang-utans live in the **rain forests** of Sumatra and Borneo. They are reddish-brown in colour and have a heavy body, with long, powerful arms and short, weak legs. Orang-utans live alone, in pairs or in small family groups. They sleep on platform nests which they make in trees. Orang-utans eat mainly fruit, but also feed on leaves, seeds, young birds and eggs.

order *noun*
An order is one of the groups that scientists use to sort, or **classify**, animals. It is the main group between **class** and **family**. **Carnivores** and **herbivores** are both examples of orders.

organ *noun*
An organ is part of an animal. An organ can be made up of one or more kinds of tissue. It always forms a complete unit with a definite part to play in the working of an animal's body. The heart is an example of an organ. Its function is to pump blood around the animal's body.

organism *noun*
An organism is any living thing. All animals and plants are organisms. Fungi are organisms, and so are the **protists** and **bacteria**, which are too tiny to be seen without a microscope.

oriole *noun*
Orioles are brightly-coloured **birds**. True orioles live in Europe, Africa, Asia and Australia, and there are 28 species. Orioles spend most of their time high in the trees, feeding on insects and fruit. They make a cup-shaped nest, woven onto a twig. Orioles have a strong, pointed bill and short, powerful legs. The males of some species have bright yellow, orange and black plumage.

oryx *noun*
Oryx are **antelope**. There are three species of oryx, two of which are endangered. Two species are found in **desert** areas of Africa. The Arabian oryx is the rarest species and lives in the desert of Saudi Arabia. The oryx has a short mane, a hump at the shoulder and large hooves. It is not a good runner, but walks for long periods to find its food. It lives on grass and shrubs, and can get all the water it needs from its food, without having to drink.

osprey *noun*
An osprey is a large **bird of prey**. There is only one species, found in all continents except South America. Ospreys live near water and feed mainly on fish. They hover over their prey. Then they plunge feet first into the water and seize the fish in their long, curved talons. Pairs of ospreys build a large nest of sticks. They use the same nest for years, and it becomes bigger as they repair it each year.

ostrich *noun*
The ostrich is the largest living **bird**. It lives in groups on sandy **plains** and open country in Africa. Ostriches are too big to fly, but they are the fastest animals to run on two legs. Ostriches eat mainly plants and fruit, but sometimes they eat small mammals and reptiles. At breeding time, one male mates with two to five females. Each female lays up to 15 eggs, all in the same shallow pit in the ground.

otter *noun*
Otters are carnivorous **mammals**. There are 12 species of otter, which belong to the **weasel** family. They are found in Europe, Asia, North America, South America and Africa. They live on coasts, or by rivers and lakes. Otters are **amphibious**, being equally at home in and out of the water. They have a slender body, with sleek, thick fur, webbed feet and a strong tail to help them swim. Otters dive well, and feed on water animals, which they come ashore to eat.

ovenbird *noun*
Ovenbirds are small **birds**. There are nearly 220 species of ovenbird, which are found in southern Mexico, Central America and South America. Ovenbirds live in a wide variety of habitats and move quickly so they are well hidden by the vegetation. They get their name from the shape of their nest, which in many species is like a small oven. It is built of mud, baked hard by the sun. Ovenbirds have a long, slender bill and eat insects, worms, seeds and fruit. Females lay from two to five eggs and both parents look after the young.

ovulation *noun*
Ovulation is the shedding of ripe **eggs** from the ovary of a female **mammal**. The female is ready to mate with the male at ovulation. If an egg is fertilized by male cells, called **sperm**, **pregnancy** happens.

owl *noun*
Owls are nocturnal **birds of prey**. There are about 145 species of owl, which are found throughout the world, and in most **habitats**. Owls have soft feathers and a short tail. Their huge eyes look forward and they have very good eyesight. Most owls hunt at night. They fly silently above their prey, and then pounce on it. Owls eat insects, birds, small rodents and rabbits. Some catch fish. Most owls have eerie, hooting calls.

oyster *noun*
Oysters are **molluscs**. They are found in all continents, in shallow, **temperate** waters. Oysters are **bivalves**, and have two uneven shells over their soft body. They feed on plankton which they strain from the sea water. Oysters live attached to rocks or to other oyster shells. Sometimes, a small object such as a grain of sand gets caught inside an oyster's shell. This irritates the oyster, and it covers it with layers of shell material to make it smooth. In this way, a pearl is made.

pampas habitat *noun*
A pampas habitat is a **habitat** which is found in South America. It is a type of **grassland**, with large, coarse grasses, such as pampas grass. In drier regions, the pampas becomes semi-desert. Animals of pampas habitats include **armadillos**, **anteaters** and **wolves**. The largest birds of the pampas are the **rheas**.

panda *noun*
Pandas are rare **mammals**. There are two species of panda, the giant panda and the red or lesser panda. They both live in bamboo forests in China. The red panda is also found in Nepal and West Burma. The giant panda has a black and white woolly coat. It eats large amounts of bamboo stems, which it grasps with its forepaws. Pandas live on the ground, but climb trees for shelter and to escape enemies. Female pandas give birth to young which are tiny, blind and helpless but develop very rapidly.

pangolin *noun*
Pangolins are **mammals** with horny, overlapping scales. There are seven species of pangolin which are found in Africa and Asia. They are also known as scaly anteaters. Some species live in trees and others on the ground. Pangolins feed at night, mainly on ants and termites. They do not have teeth, but catch their food with their long, sticky tongue. Pangolins live alone. They usually only have one baby at a time, and the baby sometimes clings on to its mother's tail. Pangolins roll themselves into a ball when threatened.

parasite noun

A parasite is an animal which lives inside or on another animal or plant. A parasite always harms the animal it lives on, called the **host**. For example, the host may suffer because the parasite is eating its food or its blood. The host does not usually die, but the parasite may carry diseases which attack the host.

parasitic adjective

A parasite which lives inside the body

A tapeworm lives inside the stomach of an animal. It hooks itself onto the wall of the stomach. It then eats the food that the host animal has digested.

A parasite which lives on the surface of the body

A flea lives on the surface of an animal's skin. It bites through the skin and feeds on the animal's blood. Only the adult flea is a parasite.

An animal which acts as a parasite

A cuckoo lays its eggs in the nest of another bird.

As the baby cuckoo grows, it pushes the other young birds out of the nest.

The host bird feeds the baby cuckoo until it is old enough to fly away.

108

panther *noun*
Panther is the name given to some
members of the **cat** family. It is normally
used to describe the black form of the
leopard. But **jaguars** and **pumas** are also
sometimes called panthers. The black
panther form of the leopard is black all over,
with the spots only showing faintly. Like their
light-coloured relatives, black panthers are
found in forests and mountains of Asia.

parasite ► page 108

parent ► page 110

parrot *noun*
Parrots are fairly large, brightly-coloured
birds. There are about 315 species of parrot
in three families. They are found in **tropical**
and sub-tropical forests throughout the
world. Parrots have a short, hooked bill,
which they use for climbing and when
feeding on fruits and seeds. Some species
also eat insects, larvae and other animals.
Many parrots live in large groups and call to
each other with loud screams. Parrots
include parakeets, budgerigars, macaws and
cockatiels.

paw *noun*
A paw is the front or rear foot of an animal.
Many animals have paws with claws. **Cats**
have paws with claws that they can pull in,
or retract.

peacock *noun*
A peacock is a male peafowl. Peafowl are
members of the **pheasant** family. They are
found in India and Sri Lanka, where they live
in forests. The peacock has glittering
feathers, a crest on his head and a beautiful,
spreading tail with spots like eyes. The
peahen is smaller. She has mostly grey-
brown plumage, and a small crest. Peafowl
feed on nuts, seeds, fruit and insects. In the
breeding season, the peacock **displays** to
the hen, spreading his tail, trailing his wings
and strutting in front of her.

peccary *noun*
Peccaries are **mammals**. They are
ungulates, and look like **pigs**, but have
longer legs. There are three species, found
in South America and Central America. They
live in tropical **rain forests**. Peccaries are
omnivorous, but prefer to eat roots, seeds
and fruits. They live in groups, and defend
their territory against other animals.
Peccaries are noisy, and make grunting
sounds, as well as laughing calls.

pelican *noun*
Pelicans are large water **birds**. There are
seven species, found by lakes and seas in
Europe, Asia, Africa, North America and
South America. Pelicans have a long bill
with a pouch made of skin hanging from it.
They live in **colonies** and feed on fish,
which they catch while they are swimming or
diving in shallow water. The females lay their
eggs in nests made of sticks.

penguin *noun*
Penguins are large sea **birds**. There are
16 species, all found in the southern
hemisphere, mostly in Antarctica and around
the southern coasts of South America and
Australia. Penguins cannot fly. Their wings
are like flat paddles and they use them for
underwater swimming. Their short legs and
webbed feet act as rudders. Penguins have
short, glossy feathers that protect them from
the cold.

parent *noun*

Parents are the male and female animals that have mated and produced **young**. Among many invertebrates, fish, amphibians and reptiles, the parents do not care for the young at all. Instead, some of these produce thousands, or even millions of eggs. Only a few of these will survive. Birds and mammals have only a few young. The parents protect and feed their offspring for months, until the young have learned to look after themselves. It is usually the female who looks after the young animal, but in some species the male helps.

The male penguin holds his mate's egg on his feet to incubate it. The egg is protected and kept warm. The male cannot fish and must feed off his body fat or blubber. When the egg hatches, the female penguin rears the chick.

Among reptiles, only crocodiles show any care as parents. The female buries her eggs in a pit and both parents guard them. When the baby crocodiles hatch, the mother takes them in her mouth and carries them to the water.

The male midwife toad looks after the eggs. He collects the strings of fertilized eggs with his back legs and hides with them in safety under a rock.

Among sticklebacks, it is the male which looks after the eggs. The male builds a nest where the female lays her eggs. He fans the eggs with fresh water and when the eggs hatch, the male guards the baby fish for about two weeks.

Scorpions are unusual among the invertebrates, because they look after their young. The baby scorpions travel around on the mother's back for a few days after they hatch.

Young mammals stay with their mother while they feed off her milk. They also learn many skills from her. This wolf has caught a rabbit. But she has let it go, so that the baby wolves can try to catch it for themselves.

perching birds *noun*
Perching birds are the largest **order** of
birds. There are more than 5,200 species of
perching bird, in about 60 families. They are
found all over the world. Perching birds
include many of the most beautiful birds, as
well as many fine songbirds. Perching birds
have feet with three toes facing forwards
and one backwards. These toes help them
to grasp thin perches, such as twigs and
grasses. **Thrushes**, **finches** and **crows** are
perching birds.

pest *noun*
Pests are animals that are harmful to other
animals or plants. Many kinds of animal can
be pests, from the simplest to the most
complicated. **Rabbits** are often regarded as
pests, because they breed rapidly and eat
the grass on which people graze their
livestock. **Locusts** are insect pests. They
can quickly strip crops bare of green leaves.

pesticide *noun*
Pesticides are chemicals that are used to
destroy **pests**. Pesticides are developed by
scientists to kill particular species of pest.
Farmers spray pesticides on to their crops
each year, to prevent damage by insect
pests. Some pesticides build up in the soil
and in animals and can poison them. Many
remain in the soil for years after they have
been put there.

petrel *noun*
Petrels are sea **birds**, related to
albatrosses. There are 78 species of petrel,
found on all the main oceans of the world.
Petrels have grey or black and white
plumage, and tube-like nostrils on their bill.
They breed in burrows, especially on
remote, rocky islands. There are two main
groups of petrel, the storm petrels and the
diving petrels. Storm petrels spend most of
their life flying over the sea, feeding on small
fish, squid and crustaceans. Diving petrels
feed by diving into the sea and swimming
under the water.

pheasant *noun*
Pheasants are plump **birds**. There are
48 species of pheasant. All of them live in
Asia, except one which lives in Africa.
Common pheasants have been introduced
to many parts of the world, including Europe,
North America and Australia. Many species
of pheasant live on seeds which they scratch
for on the ground with their thick legs and
strong claws. Many male pheasants have
bright, colourful plumage, and a long,
curved tail.

phylum (plural **phyla**) *noun*
A phylum is one of the groups that scientists
use to sort, or **classify**, animals. It is the
main group between **kingdom** and **class**.
There are about 33 phyla in the animal
kingdom. Some phyla include many
thousands of species, and others very few.
The animals in one phylum share the same
type of body. **Molluscs**, **roundworms** and
arthropods are all examples of animal
phyla.

pig *noun*
Pigs are large **mammals**. They are found in
Asia, Africa and Europe. The best-known
pigs are the wild boar of Europe and Asia
and the warthog of Africa. Pigs have a
plump body and short legs with hooves.
They live in family groups and dig in the soil
for roots using their upturned teeth.

pigeon *noun*
Pigeons are medium-sized **birds**. There are about 300 species in the pigeon family, which also includes doves. They are found in all parts of the world except in the north of North America and northern Asia. Pigeons can fly very fast. Female pigeons lay one or two white eggs in a **nest** made of sticks. They eat seeds and fruit and have soft, cooing calls.

pigment *noun*
Pigment is a coloured chemical which is found in the body of animals. **Fur, feathers, skin** and other tissues are all coloured by pigments. For example, the pigment in the fur of a red squirrel gives it a rusty brown colour. Animals without pigment in their body are called **albino**.

pincer *noun*
Pincers are enlarged, gripping claws on the limbs of some kinds of animal. **Lobsters, crabs** and **scorpions** have pincers on one pair of feet to help them grasp their prey, or to frighten off their enemies.

pipit *noun*
Pipits are small **birds**. They belong to the same family as wagtails and there are about 40 species. Pipits have long claws, brown, streaky plumage and clear, piping calls. They live in heathy and grassy **habitats**, where they eat insects and build a **nest** from woven grasses.

piranha *noun*
Piranhas are **fish**. There are about 25 species of piranha. They live in the warm, tropical streams of South America, where they swim in shoals. Piranhas are mainly **carnivores**. They have sharp teeth which they use to tear flesh from other animals.

pit viper *noun*
Pit vipers are **reptiles**. There are about 140 species of pit viper, which are related to **vipers** and **rattlesnakes**. Pit vipers have a hole, or pit, inside their head, which leads to a group of special **cells**. These cells can detect heat. When hunting, pit vipers can sense the body heat given off by small mammals and birds and strike at them with their poisonous fangs, even in darkness.

plains habitat *noun*
Plains habitats are flat areas of land found on every continent. Some plains are covered in trees or scrub, others are grassy. Some are hot and dry like deserts, others are always covered in snow and ice. Coastal plains usually lie at a lower altitude than the rest of the land. Mountain plains are at a high altitude.

plankton *noun*
Plankton is the name used for all the tiny animals and plants which drift in the sea. Plankton includes algae, and small animals such as the larvae of **crustaceans, molluscs** and **fish**. Although some kinds of plankton can swim, they are usually swept about by the ocean currents.

platypus *noun*
The platypus is a **monotreme mammal**. The single species lives in streams in eastern Australia. It has webbed feet, a beak like a duck and a long, furry body. The male platypus has a poisonous spur on its hind legs. Like other monotremes, the female platypus lays **eggs**. Platypuses use their bill to scoop up worms, shellfish and other small animals from the bottom of streams.

plover *noun*
Plovers are **birds**. There are about 62 species of plover, that are found on sea-shores all over the world. Plovers have a short beak, a short body and long legs. They often nest on the open ground amongst stones and pebbles. The female usually lays four eggs which are spotted brown and well **camouflaged**. Young plovers leave the nest soon after hatching and they can soon run and feed on their own.

plumage *noun*
Plumage is the covering of **feathers** found on all **birds**. Some birds, such as female **ducks** and **pheasants**, have very drab, brown plumage. Others, such as the male **bird of paradise**, and the male **peacock**, have very bright and gaudy plumage.

plume feather ► **feather**

poison *noun*
Poison is a substance which attacks the body of an animal or a plant. Many animals make poison in their body to protect themselves from attack, or to kill their prey. Some **fish** have poisonous spines, and many **snakes** have a poisonous bite.

polar bear *noun*
A polar bear is a large, strong **mammal**. There is only one species of polar bear, which lives in areas around the North Pole. It is the largest **carnivore** that lives on land. Polar bears have thick white or yellowish fur, and layers of fat in their skin, to protect them from the cold. They swim well and feed mainly on seals.

polar habitat *noun*
Polar habitats are areas which lie within or close to the Arctic and Antarctic circles. These habitats are very cold for most of the year, and much of the surface is covered in snow or ice. In summer, the days are long, but the winters are very dark. Some animals found in polar habitats **hibernate** during the winter. Others **migrate** to warmer regions.

polecat *noun*
Polecats are small **mammals**. There are three species of polecat, which belong to the **weasel** family. Polecats live in Europe and Asia. They have a long body with bold black and white markings. Polecats live in woodland, steppe and semi-deserts, where they hunt small mammals and birds.

polyp *noun*
A polyp is a soft-bodied stage in the life cycle of jellyfish, sea anemones and corals. Polyps have tentacles and they attach themselves like plants to the sea-bed. In the middle of the tentacles is the mouth of the polyp. In some species, such as **corals**, the polyps are joined together to make a **colony**. In others, such as **sea anemones**, the polyps are single.

population *noun*
A population is a group of animals of the same **species**, which lives together in the same **habitat** and which breeds together. In some species of animal, populations remain in the same area. In other species, populations **migrate** or move about over a wide area.

porcupine *noun*
Porcupines are **mammals**. There are two different families of porcupine. In the New World family, there are 10 species, which live in North and South America. In the Old World family, there are 11 species. They live in Europe, Africa and Asia. Porcupines are large **rodents**, with long, sharp spines. American porcupines have a long tail and can climb trees well. Old World porcupines live on the ground and dig **burrows**.

porpoise *noun*
Porpoises are fish-shaped **mammals**. There are six species of porpoise. Porpoises live mainly in the temperate seas of the Northern hemisphere, in the Indian and western Pacific Oceans and off the coast of southern South America. They look like small whales, and their front limbs are **flippers**. Porpoises have a rounded snout, and a small number of flat teeth. They feed on small fish and squid.

possum *noun*
Possums are small or medium-sized **mammals**. There are about 40 species of possum, found in Australia and New Guinea. The common brushtail possum has been introduced to New Zealand. Possums have soft fur and a long tail. They climb well and spend a lot of time in trees. They feed on leaves, fruit and insects. The tiny honey possum of south-west Australia feeds only on the nectar of flowers.

posterior *adjective*
Posterior describes the rear part of an animal, or any part which is positioned at the back. The opposite of posterior is **anterior**.

potto *noun*
A potto is a **mammal**. It is in the group of **primates**, together with **monkeys**, **apes** and humans. Pottos live in the tropical forests of West Africa. They are active only at night. Pottos climb slowly in the trees, often upside down, gripping with their feet. They feed on fruit, and sometimes also on small birds and mammals.

pouch *noun*
A pouch is a flap of skin on the lower belly of an adult female animal. It is a special feature, or **characteristic**, of **marsupial mammals**. When a young marsupial is born, it clambers into the safety of its mother's pouch, where it feeds on **milk**. Young **kangaroos** use the pouch as a safe place for several months, returning to it when danger threatens.

prairie dog *noun*
Prairie dogs are small **mammals**. There are five species of prairie dog, which are found in Mexico and the USA. They belong to the **squirrel** family, but have a shorter tail than tree-living squirrels. Prairie dogs live in **colonies**, in underground **burrows**. They graze on open **grasslands** and dash into their burrows if they spot any danger.

predator *noun*

A predator is an animal that hunts and eats other animals. Many predators have sharp teeth and claws, a sticky tongue or a poisonous bite or sting. Some animals catch their prey with a lure. Predatory animals may hunt alone, as **cheetahs** do, or they may hunt in groups, as **wolves** do. **Camouflage** is useful for many predators. Their victims cannot see them easily. When they catch prey, the predators may eat it at once or they may take it away to share with a family group.

The chameleon waits for an insect to land nearby. Then it slowly creeps up on its prey. When it is near enough, it catches the insect with its sticky tongue. Its tongue is longer than its body and tail.

The bolas spider spins a single thread of silk with a tiny drop of glue at one end. When an insect flies past, the spider throws the weighted thread so that it hits and sticks to the prey.

The anglerfish uses a lure to attract fish to it. It has a long piece of flesh that looks like food and dangles over its mouth. When another fish tries to bite the lure, the anglerfish opens its mouth and sucks its prey in.

The cheetah can run faster than any other animal, over short distances. It uses stealth and camouflage to stalk its prey and then chases it.

The rattlesnake uses its poisonous bite to stun its victim. It sinks its special teeth called fangs into its victim. It injects venom into the body of its prey and soon the animal cannot move.

This killer whale beats its powerful tail to help it lunge out of the water and onto a beach. It seizes a seal pup in its strong jaws.

prairie habitat *noun*
The prairie habitat is a **habitat** of wide-open areas of **grassland**. The prairie once stretched for hundreds of kilometres across the central plains of the United States of America. Now it is mostly used for growing crops, but small parts have been made into nature reserves. Animals found in the prairie habitat include **prairie dogs**, **deer**, **coyotes** and many kinds of bird, such as **grouse** and **larks**.

predator ► page 116

pregnancy ► gestation

prehensile *adjective*
Prehensile describes a **tail** which can be used to grasp. Many **monkeys** have a prehensile tail. They use this as a fifth limb when they are climbing and swinging in the branches of trees. Some **mice**, such as the harvest mouse, have a prehensile tail to help them balance amongst grass stalks.

prehistoric *adjective*
Prehistoric describes a time before human history, which began only about 40,000 years ago. Many animals lived in prehistoric times, and they are called prehistoric animals. The **dinosaurs** are the most famous of all prehistoric animals. They lived about 100 million years ago. Other prehistoric animals are **ammonites**, **mammoths** and **sabre-toothed cats**. The oldest prehistoric animals lived in the sea over 600 million years ago.

prey *noun*
Prey are animals which form food for other animals, called **predators**. For example, mice are prey for **carnivorous** animals such as foxes and owls. Insects are the prey of many species of mammal and bird. Many **marine** animals depend on fish and the larvae of invertebrates as their prey.

primary feather ► feather

primate *noun*
Primates are a group of **mammals**. There are 183 species of primate. They include lemurs, pottos, tarsiers, marmosets, monkeys, apes, and humans. Primates include the most intelligent of all animals. They have hands and feet with grasping thumbs and toes, a large brain and forward-facing eyes with **binocular vision**.

proboscis *noun*
A proboscis is a pointed part of an animal's head. Many **insects** have a proboscis, which they use for sucking up liquid food. An **aphid** uses its proboscis to suck the sap from a plant. The long nose of **mammals**, such as **tapirs**, **elephants** and elephant **seals**, is also known as a proboscis.

protist *noun*
Protists are tiny living things, or **organisms**. They are found in land and water all over the world. Most protists are too small to be seen without a microscope. They have a simple form. Protists sometimes have a kind of tail called a flagellum, which pushes them along. Scientists think that all animals, plants and fungi **evolved** from protists.

pterodactyl *noun*
Pterodactyls were flying **reptiles**. They lived about 200 million years ago and are now **extinct**. They had a long, horny beak and pointed, leathery wings. They probably fed on fish. Unlike birds, pterodactyls had no feathers. They moved through the air more by gliding than by flapping their wings.

pufferfish *noun*
Pufferfish are small **fish**. There are about 120 species, many of which live in warm **tropical** seas and on coral reefs. Other species are found in brackish and fresh water. Pufferfish have a hard, beak-like mouth. When threatened, they can blow up their bodies with water to many times their normal size. Many species of pufferfish have a poisonous body.

puffin *noun*
Puffins are **birds**. There are three species of puffin, which belong to the same family as guillemots. Puffins have a rounded body, black and white plumage and a large, brightly-coloured bill. They nest in burrows on cliff-tops or on lonely, rocky islands. Puffins feed on small fish and sandeels.

pupa *noun*
A pupa is a stage in the development, or **metamorphosis**, of many **insects**. The pupa is the resting stage between the caterpillar or larva, and the adult insect. In butterflies and moths, a pupa is sometimes called a **chrysalis** or, if it is covered in silk, a **cocoon**. The larva feeds and grows, then fixes itself in a safe spot. Its skin hardens and forms a case. Inside the case, the pupa changes from a crawling larva into a fully formed adult insect.
pupate *verb*

python *noun*
Pythons are **reptiles**. They are non-poisonous **snakes**. There are seven species of python, and they belong to the same family as **boas**. The largest pythons grow up to about 10 metres long. Pythons wrap their thick, muscular body round and suffocate their prey before eating it. They feed mainly on mammals and birds.

puma *noun*
A puma is a large **mammal**. It is a species of **cat**. Pumas live in North and South America, in all kinds of **habitats**, from mountain woodland to grassland, desert and tropical forests. Pumas are normally grey-brown in colour, but they are occasionally black. They grow up to about 2.75 metres long, including the tail. Pumas eat mainly other mammals, from small rodents up to adult deer. A puma is also called a cougar, a mountain lion or a panther.

Q

R

quadruped *noun*
Quadrupeds are **animals** which move on four legs. Many mammals walk, run or jump on all fours. Examples of mammal quadrupeds include mice, pigs, horses and elephants. Most **reptiles** and **amphibians** are also quadrupeds.

queen ► **social insect**

quetzal *noun*
The quetzal, or resplendent quetzal, is a **bird**. It lives in the tropical **rain forests** of Central and South America and feeds mainly on fruit. Quetzals belong to the trogon family. They have bright green plumage, with a red belly. The male quetzal has a feathery, flowing tail, up to a metre long.

rabbit *noun*
Rabbits are medium-sized **mammals**. They belong to the same family as **hares**. Rabbits are found all over the world, in most **habitats**. There are 17 species of rabbit, including the cottontails of North America. Rabbits have large ears and a short tail. They use their long back legs to hop around and dig in the soil.

raccoon *noun*
Raccoons are **mammals**. There are six species of raccoon, all found in North and South America. Coatis and **pandas** are in the same family as raccoons. The common raccoon has been introduced to some parts of Europe and Asia. Raccoons have a long tail and black, mask-like face markings. They are most active at night, when they hunt for a variety of prey, including insects, rodents, fruit, nuts, frogs and fish. Raccoons often raid dustbins to search for food.

ragworm *noun*
Ragworms are soft-bodied **worms**. They belong to the **phylum** of segmented worms, together with **earthworms** and **leeches**. Ragworms live in the sea, or on the sea-bed. They have a tube-shaped body, divided into rings. Some ragworms swim in the sea, using their paddle-shaped bristles. Others lurk in burrows in soft sand or mud.

rail *noun*
Rails are small **birds**. There are 124 species of rail, found all over the world. They have long legs and short, rounded wings. Most rails have dull brown or grey plumage and many live in wet **habitats**. Many species live only on islands, and some of these island rails cannot fly. The corncrake and the common moorhen are kinds of rail.

rain forest habitat *noun*
Rain forest habitats are the richest **habitats** in the world. They are found in the warm tropics, especially around large rivers such as the Amazon in South America and the Congo in Africa. South-east Asia and Australia also have areas of tropical rain forest. The trees in a rain forest grow very tall, and the undergrowth is also lush. This means that the floor of the forest is shady. A huge variety of animals and plants lives in rain forest habitats.

rare ► page 122

rat *noun*
Rats are small, furry **mammals**. There are about 120 species of rat, in the same family as **mice**. Rats are large, active **rodents**. They have a thin, scaly tail and long, sharp claws. They feed on a great variety of food, including grain, seeds, fruit and insects. The brown rat and the black or roof rat have become common pests. They can be found in drains and buildings all over the world. The largest rat is the giant pouched rat of West Africa. It is about 37 centimetres long.

rat opossum *noun*
Rat or shrew opossums are small **marsupial mammals**. There are seven species of rat opossum. They are found in the Andes mountains of South America. Rat opossums are about 25 centimetres long, including the tail which is about as long as the body. They have a pointed nose and sharp teeth, which they use to kill their prey of insects.

ratel *noun*
A ratel is a short-legged, stocky **mammal**. It is sometimes called the honey badger and belongs to the **weasel** family. Ratels live in Africa and Asia, in **forest** or **savanna** habitats. They have sharp claws and strong jaws, which they use to break open bees' nests in trees to feed on the honey. They often use a bird called the **honeyguide** to lead them to a bees' nest. The bird eats its share of honey after the ratel has broken open the nest.

rattlesnake *noun*
Rattlesnakes are **reptiles**. They are large, poisonous **snakes**. Rattlesnakes belong to the same family as **vipers** and **pit vipers**. Like pit vipers, rattlesnakes have special **cells** in their head. They use these cells to sense the body heat of their prey. When they are disturbed, rattlesnakes make a rattling sound by shaking loose scales at the tip of their tail.

rare   *adjective*

Rare describes something that is not often seen or found. Some species of animal are rare and there are very few animals alive. Animals may become rare because their **habitat** is being destroyed by pollution or for farming. Or the animal may be hunted for food, for its skin or for its horns. Some species have even become **extinct** which means there are no more animals of that species left alive. **Conservation** plans try to protect rare animals and help them survive.

There are several thousand species of rare animal. Here are some of them.

There are probably several hundred golden lion tamarins left. This primate lives in the rain forests of Brazil. Much of this forest has been cleared for building. Tamarins have also been captured for pets.

The tropical hawksbill turtle provides beautiful, patterned tortoiseshell for ornaments and jewellery. It has been hunted so much that it is nearly extinct.

The hyacinth macaw from Brazil has become rare because its habitat is being destroyed. Also, like many parrots, it is captured and sold as a pet. Each year, up to 1,000 of these macaws are smuggled out of Brazil to become pets.

There are only a few thousand blue whales alive in the world's oceans. For hundreds of years, this magnificent mammal has been hunted for its oil and its fat, called blubber.

The Arabian oryx is a small antelope. This animal has been hunted for its coat, its long, delicate horns and its meat. No wild Arabian oryx have been seen since 1972, but some zoo-bred animals have been returned to the wild in Oman.

The white rhino is extremely rare. Very few are left in their natural habitat, the African savanna. They are rare because they are killed illegally for their horn. Rhino horn is used to make jewellery, ornaments and in local medicine.

ray *noun*
Rays are large fish. They have a flat body, wing-like fins and a long tail. Like sharks, rays are **cartilaginous fish**. This means their skeleton is made of cartilage instead of bone. Rays often lie still on the sea-bed, then flap off through the water to a fresh spot. Many rays have sharp spines along their back, and in some species these carry poisonous stings.

regeneration *noun*
Regeneration is the way an animal replaces or renews part of its body. The **cells** which make up animals are being broken down and replaced all the time, and this is called regeneration. Regeneration of tissues causes wounds to heal. Regeneration of bones causes them to mend when they are broken. Many animals, such as **worms** and **reptiles**, can regenerate large parts of their body.
regenerate *verb*

regurgitate *verb*
Regurgitate describes the way an animal brings undigested food back into its mouth. **Ruminant** animals, such as **deer** and **giraffes**, regurgitate their food as part of their normal method of eating. They chew the regurgitated food and swallow it again. This helps ruminants to **digest** tough leaves and grasses.

reindeer ▶ **caribou**

reproduction *noun*
Reproduction is the making of **young**, or **offspring**. Simple animals can reproduce by splitting their body in two. This is called **asexual reproduction**. In most complicated animals, reproduction is **sexual**, when male **sperms** join together with a female **egg**. The young that are made by sexual reproduction are not the same as their parents. Their genes are different.

reptile ▶ page 126

rhea *noun*
Rheas are large, flightless **birds**. There are two species of rhea, both found in central South America. They live in grassy and scrubby **habitats**. Rheas have brown feathers and a long, white neck. They run fast on their long, strong legs. Unlike most birds, the male rhea looks after the eggs in the nest. There can be up to 60 eggs, laid by many different females. The male also cares for the baby rheas.

rhinoceros *noun*
Rhinoceroses are large **mammals**. The five species live in grasslands in Africa and South-east Asia. They have very tough skin and short, thick legs, with hoofed feet. On the front of their head, rhinoceroses have one or two long, curved horns made of compressed hair. Rhinoceroses feed on grass and twigs. They need to drink a lot of water and usually live near a river or pond.

ribbon worm *noun*

Ribbon worms, or nemertines, are broad, flat **worms**. There are about 900 species of ribbon worm. Nearly all species live in the sea. Some are found in fresh water and a few live on land. All ribbon worms have a long **proboscis** in the gut, which can be pushed out through an opening at the end of the body. They use the proboscis to catch prey, in defence and to help them move. Many ribbon worms are very small, but one species can reach a length of over 30 metres, even longer than a blue whale!

ringtail *noun*

Ringtails are small, furry **mammals**. There are about 22 species of ringtail, all found in the forests of Australia and New Guinea. They have large eyes, a pointed nose, short legs and a long, furry tail. Their tail is **prehensile**, and they use it to help them climb amongst the trees. Two species of ringtail have special skin, or membrane, between their legs and body and can glide through the air. Ringtails eat sap from trees, plants and leaves.

river dolphin *noun*

River dolphins are water **mammals**. The five species are in the same family as **porpoises** and **killer whales**. They are found in rivers in South America and Asia. River dolphins have a streamlined body, rounded forehead and long, slender beak. They have little or no eyesight and rely on **echo-location** to find food in the muddy water of the rivers in which they live. They eat fish and small crustaceans.

roach *noun*

The roach is a freshwater **fish**. It belongs to the same family as carp and minnows. Roach live in lakes and rivers of Europe and western Asia. They have a deep body which is silver-coloured with a greenish back. Their lower fins are red. Roach eat a variety of food, such as insects, larvae, crustaceans and plants.

rodent *noun*

Rodents are **mammals**. They form the most widespread and largest **order** of mammals, with about 1,700 species. Rodents include **rats**, **mice** and **squirrels**. Nearly all rodents are small animals, and most are **nocturnal**. Some rodents burrow, some climb trees and others are good swimmers. Rodents have long teeth in their upper and lower jaws which grow throughout their life. The teeth are kept short by the animals' gnawing action as they feed. Most rodents are herbivores, but some are omnivores.

roundworm *noun*

Roundworms, or nematodes, are **invertebrate** animals. There are about 10,000 species of roundworm, found in all **habitats** all over the world. They have a rounded, tapered body, without separate segments. It is blunt at the front and pointed at the rear. There are some species of roundworm which live as **parasites** inside the body of other animals.

ruminant *noun*

Ruminants are hoofed **mammals** which chew their food twice. There are about 170 species of ruminant, including sheep, goats, antelope, deer and giraffes. A ruminant feeds on grass and tough plant material. It swallows the partly chewed stalks into the first stomach, or rumen, where they are partly **digested**. The animal then brings back, or **regurgitates**, the food into the mouth. Here it is chewed again, swallowed and then properly digested.

reptile   *noun*

A reptile is a **vertebrate** with dry, scaly skin. The skin forms a protective armour. Reptiles are a **class** of animals and scientists have named about 6,000 **species**. Most reptiles, such as **crocodiles**, **alligators** and **turtles**, have four legs and a tail. Some, such as **snakes** and some **lizards**, have no legs. Reptiles are **cold-blooded**, so they become inactive in cold weather and may **hibernate**. Although reptiles live in most parts of the world, they are most common in **tropical** regions. Most reptiles live on land. The ones that live at sea do not breathe under water. Reptiles have **lungs** to breathe.

Many reptiles, such as turtles, mate once a year. Reptiles produce young by sexual reproduction. The male reptile fertilizes the egg inside the female's body.

shell

front flipper

eye

nostril

mouth

back flipper

This is a fully-grown turtle.

Most reptiles lay eggs. Some keep the eggs inside their body and produce live young. Reptile eggs are either leathery or hard, so that water inside cannot seep out. Once they are laid, the eggs are abandoned by the parents. The heat from the Sun incubates them.

When the young are ready to hatch, they break through the shell, using the spike on their snout, called the egg tooth.

The young reptiles must look after themselves. Most young reptiles receive no care from their parents. These young turtles face many dangers on their journey to the sea.

The young reptiles look just like small adults and they can do everything the adults can do.

S

sable *noun*
A sable is a small **mammal**. It belongs to the **weasel** family and is related to **martens**. The sable lives in the north of Asia and Japan. It has thick, dark fur and a short, bushy tail. The sable lives on the ground in **forest habitats**. It feeds on small mammals as well as on fish, insects, honey and fruits. Sables live alone. The babies, known as kits, are born nearly naked, blind and deaf. They stay in the nest until they are about three months old.

sabre-toothed cat *noun*
Sabre-toothed cats, or sabre-toothed tigers, were **prehistoric** mammals. They lived until about two million years ago. Sabre-toothed cats were **carnivores**. They had a pair of very long teeth in their upper jaw, and strong neck muscles. Scientists think that they killed other mammals by stabbing them with these sharp teeth.

sac *noun*
A sac is a pouch inside the body of an animal. It often contains liquid.

salamander *noun*
Salamanders are **amphibians**. There are about 350 species of salamander, including **newts**. Salamanders are found in many parts of the world. Some live most of their life on land and others in water, but they all **breed** in or near water. Salamanders have strong limbs and moveable eyelids. They are **carnivores** and eat mostly small invertebrates. Lungless salamanders breathe entirely through their skin.

salmon *noun*
Salmon are river **fish**. There are about 70 species in the salmon family, which also includes chars and graylings. Some salmon spend most of their life in the sea and others in fresh water, but they all **spawn** in fresh water. Salmon do not have scales on their head, and have a fatty fin on their back. The female salmon lays her eggs in a shallow nest on the gravel bed of the river, where they are **fertilized**. The young salmon hatch the following spring.

salt marsh habitat *noun*
Salt marsh habitats are wet **habitats** near the sea. They are mostly found in the cooler and drier parts of the world. At high tide, the sea covers the salt marshes so that the soil is always very wet and salty. Animals which live in salt marsh habitats have to survive conditions which change suddenly from wet to dry. They also have to be able to deal with a lot of salt in their diet. Many **birds** feed or roost on salt marshes.

sandgrouse *noun*
Sandgrouse are long-tailed **birds**. There are 16 species of sandgrouse and they live in Asia, Africa and southern Europe. They are found in **deserts** and other very dry habitats. Sandgrouse have sandy-coloured plumage and are well **camouflaged** on the ground. They eat desert plants. Female sandgrouse lay their eggs in a shallow nest on the ground. The male sandgrouse carries water to the young birds by soaking his belly feathers in a pond or stream and then flying back to the nest.

sandpiper *noun*
Sandpipers are shore **birds**. There are
about 80 species in the sandpiper family,
which also includes snipes, curlews and
godwits. Sandpipers have long wings and a
short tail. Many species also have long legs
and bill, and several have a curved bill. Like
other **waders**, sandpipers find their food in
the water, or in wet mud or sand. They eat
worms and small crustaceans. Most
sandpipers **breed** in the northern part of the
world. They **migrate** south in the autumn to
feed on estuaries and sea-shores.

savanna habitat *noun*
A savanna habitat is a type of **grassland
habitat**, which is found mainly in **tropical**
regions of Africa. In a savanna habitat, the
vegetation is made up of long grasses, with
scattered trees and bushes. Grass fires are
common in savannas during the dry season.
Some **mammals** of the savanna are
gazelles, cheetahs, elephants and zebras.
Large birds, such as ostriches, secretary
birds and bustards, are also at home in a
savanna habitat.

scale *noun*
Scales are thin plates on the skin of an
animal. **Reptiles** have scales to stop them
from drying out so they can live on land.
Their scales are made of horny material.
Birds have scales on their legs and feet.
The soft body of a **fish** is protected by bony
scales.

scavenger *noun*
Scavengers are animals which live on the
dead bodies of other animals, or **carrion**.
Scavengers do not kill their own prey, but
watch out for animals which have been killed
by other **predators**, or which have died.
Examples of scavengers are **hyenas** and
vultures. Vultures scavenge by soaring over
open country and looking for dead animals
on the ground below.

scent ► **nose**

scorpion *noun*
Scorpions are **arthropods**. There are about
1,200 species, in the same group as
spiders, **mites** and **ticks**. A scorpion has
eight legs and strong claws called pincers.
Its long tail has a poisonous sting at its tip
and arches forward over the scorpion's
back. Most scorpions live in hot, dry
climates. They come out at night to feed on
insects and spiders, as well as small lizards
and mice.

scorpion fish *noun*
Scorpion fish are spiny **fish** found in shallow
seas. There are about 330 species in the
scorpion fish family, which also includes
rockfish and redfish. Scorpion fish have a
very spiny body and fins. The fin spines are
poisonous and predators learn to avoid
eating these fish. Scorpion fish hide
amongst seaweed, well **camouflaged** by
their mottled colours.

sea anemone *noun*
Sea anemones are **invertebrate** animals.
They are found in all the seas of the world.
Many sea anemones are brightly coloured
and look like flowers. Sea anemones have a
ring of tentacles around their mouth. They
use their tentacles to catch small animals to
eat. They can also feed on larger animals,
such as crabs and fish. Most adult sea
anemones live attached to rocks, but some
can swim.

sea cucumber *noun*
Sea cucumbers are **invertebrate** animals,
related to **starfish**. There are about
500 species of sea cucumber, found in all
the oceans. Sea cucumbers have a long,
tube-shaped body and a ring of tentacles
round their mouth. Sea cucumbers burrow
into the sandy bottom of the sea. Some
species poison their prey, and others feed by
picking up bits of food from the sea-bed with
their sticky tentacles.

sea horse *noun*
Sea horses are marine **fish**. There are
about 25 species. Sea horses swim upright,
with their horse-like head held pointing
forwards at a sharp angle. They use their
curly tail to cling on to seaweeds, and their
body is patterned and coloured like the
plants. Sea horses swim slowly by fanning
their back fin. They feed on larvae and small
crustaceans. The female sea horse
produces 50 or more eggs which the male
then **incubates** in a special pouch.

sea lion *noun*
Sea lions are marine **mammals**. There are
14 species in the family, which also contains
fur **seals**. They live in the Atlantic, Indian
and Pacific oceans. They have outer ears
and can tuck their hind flippers under their
heavy body to help them to walk on land.
Sea lions are **carnivorous** and eat fish,
squid and penguins. Male sea lions are
much larger than the females, and have a
shaggy mane of fur around their neck, like a
male lion.

sea snake *noun*
Sea snakes are poisonous **snakes**. Most
species of sea snake are found in the
shallow seas of the south-west Pacific
Ocean, but one also lives in the Indian
Ocean. They have a flattened tail to help
them swim underwater and nostrils which
they can close. Sea snakes have highly
poisonous **venom**, but they are not usually
aggressive towards people. Most species
spend all their life in the sea and give birth to
live young.

sea lily *noun*
Sea lilies, or feather stars, are **invertebrate**
animals. There are about 625 species of sea
lily, found in seas all over the world. They
are related to **starfish**. Sea lilies have long,
feathery arms which they use to filter small
particles of food from the sea water. They
have five main arms, but these may branch
many times. Some sea lilies live attached to
the sea-bed or to a plant by a long stalk.
Others float freely in the water.

sea spider *noun*
Sea spiders are marine **arthropods**. There
are about 1,000 species of sea spider, found
in most seas of the world. Sea spiders have
a small body and long, jointed legs. Most
species have eight legs, but some have
10 or 12. Sea spiders feed on soft-bodied
invertebrates and are often found clinging to
their prey. They have pincers which they use
to hold the prey or to tear off pieces of food.

sea urchin   *noun*
Sea urchins are **invertebrate** animals.
There are about 950 species of sea urchin,
found in all the oceans. They have a round
body, covered in sharp, moveable spines.
Most species have pincers on long stalks.
They use these pincers for defence, to clean
between their spines and for feeding. Sea
urchins eat mostly algae, but may also eat
small animals that live on the bottom of the
ocean.

sea-bed habitat   *noun*
A sea-bed habitat is a **habitat** which is found
at the bottom of the sea. It may be muddy,
sandy or rocky. The water above the sea-
bed is very deep in parts of the oceans, but
is shallow around continents and islands. In
the deep oceans, the sea-bed is very dark.
Examples of animals which live on the sea-
bed are **worms**, **molluscs** and some kinds
of **fish**.

seal   *noun*
Seals are marine **mammals**. There are
19 species of seal. Most live in the seas, but
a few live in fresh water. Seals have a
torpedo-shaped body and a thick layer of
fatty **blubber** just under their furry skin.
Unlike **sea lions**, they do not have outer
ears and they cannot walk easily on land.
They swim and dive well, using sideways
movements of their body. Seals are
carnivorous, and dive to catch fish,
crustaceans and other food.

sea-shore habitat   *noun*
A sea-shore habitat is a **habitat** which is
found where the land meets the sea. Some
sea-shores are rocky, with rock pools which
fill up when the tide comes in. Other sea-
shores have sandy, pebbly or muddy
beaches which slope down into the water.
Animals of the sea-shore include wading
birds, and many kinds of small
invertebrates, such as molluscs, worms
and starfish.

season   *noun*
A season is a part of the year. In **tropical**
areas, all the seasons are the same. In
temperate regions, each season has a
particular kind of weather. Summer is the
warmest season, with the longest days.
Winter is the coldest season, with the
shortest days. Spring and autumn may be
long or short seasons, depending on how far
the land is from the poles. Animals and
plants are adapted to live in the different
conditions of each season.

secondary feather ► feather

secretary bird   *noun*
A secretary bird is a **bird of prey**. It lives in
Africa. The secretary bird has long legs and
a long tail. It spends most of its time on the
ground, striding over the open country. It is
carnivorous and eats reptiles, small
mammals and insects. The name secretary
bird comes from the crest which is said to
look like the old-fashioned quill pens once
worn by a lawyer's clerk.

secrete   *verb*
A secretion is a substance which passes out
from a special **cell** in an animal's body. All
cells secrete some substances, but most
secretions come from gland cells. A
hormone called insulin is secreted by the
pancreas and helps to **digest** sugar. The
cells lining the nose secrete **mucus**, which
stops dust getting into the lungs.
secretion   *noun*

segment *noun*
A segment is a section of an animal's body.
Earthworms are made up of many
segments, which look like rings on the
surface. Each segment contains blood
vessels, nerves and organs for getting rid of
waste. The segments at the front end of a
segmented animal form the head. They are
often very different from those further down
the body. Some animals **reproduce** by
segmentation, or budding off, segments from
their bodies.

sense *noun*
A sense is the means an animal uses to find
out what is going on around it. Animals react
to temperature, light, sound or movement in
their **environment**. The main senses are
sight, hearing, taste, smell and touch. There
are special sense **organs** for each sense.
These are the eyes, the ears, the mouth, the
nose and the skin. Messages from the sense
organs travel through the **nerves** to the
brain of the animal. The sense organs of
arthropods are the **antennae**.

serval *noun*
A serval is a small **mammal**. It is a slender,
long-legged **cat** found in Africa. The serval
has a small head, a short tail and rounded
ears. It can hear and see very well. A serval
is pale brown in colour, with black spots. It
lives on the **savanna** and in lightly wooded
areas. Servals hunt small mammals,
including rodents and small antelopes, but
they also eat birds, lizards and insects. They
usually live alone. Females raise two or
three young in a den or a burrow taken over
from another animal.

sexual reproduction *noun*
Sexual reproduction is reproduction which
requires two parents. In sexual reproduction,
male sex cells or **sperm** join with female sex
cells or **eggs**. This is called **fertilization**.
Young animals develop from the fertilized
eggs. The opposite of sexual reproduction is
asexual reproduction.

shark *noun*
Shark are **cartilaginous fish**. There are
about 350 species in the shark family, which
also includes **dogfish**. They are found in
seas throughout the world. Sharks have
sharp teeth in both jaws, rough skin, stiff fins
and a streamlined tail. They range in size
from less than a metre to about 15 metres.
They eat many kinds of aquatic animal,
including fish, dolphins and seals. The
largest shark, the whale shark, filters tiny
animals from the water.

shell ► page 133

shellfish *noun*
Shellfish are **invertebrate** animals. They live
in the sea and have a **shell** or hard, outer
skeleton. Shellfish have many different
shapes and sizes. **Molluscs**, such as
periwinkles, limpets and mussels, are
shellfish. Some **crustaceans**, such as crabs
and shrimps, are also called shellfish.
Shellfish is not a scientific term, and these
animals are not fish at all.

shrew *noun*
Shrews are small **mammals**. There are
about 250 species of shrew. They are found
all over the world except in the polar regions
and Australia. Shrews have a long, pointed
nose and a long tail. The pygmy shrew is
one of the smallest known mammals. It is
only about nine centimetres long, including
the tail. Most shrews live in grassland or
woodland where they scurry about,
searching for insects and worms. They have
a keen sense of smell and hearing, but poor
eyesight.

shell *noun*

A shell is the hard, outer covering of animals such as **snails**, **beetles** and **lobsters**. Many **invertebrates** grow shells to protect their soft body. Shells can be made of **chitin**. In some animals, such as the snail, the shell is part of the body and it gets bigger as the animal grows. Other animals, such as the **crab**, have rigid shells. The shell cannot expand as the crab grows, so the crab must **moult** its shell regularly.

As the nautilus grows, its adds another box to the end of its shell. The nautilus lives in the outside box.

The hermit crab does not grow a shell of its own. It lives inside an empty mollusc shell. As the hermit crab gets bigger, it moves into a bigger shell. This hermit crab is moving into a whelk shell.

A horseshoe crab has a rigid shell. This crab has moulted its hard shell and has a soft covering. This will soon harden.

shrike   *noun*

Shrikes are **perching birds**. There are
70 species of shrike, found in Africa,
Europe, Asia and North America. They live
in areas with tall grasses and open spaces
with scattered bushes. Shrikes have a
sharp, hooked bill and strong legs with sharp
claws. Shrikes are very fierce birds. They
behave like miniature birds of prey, catching
large insects, and small birds and mammals,
by swooping down suddenly. Some shrikes
make a larder by hanging their prey on
thorns or in the branches of trees. This habit
has given them the name of butcherbird.

shrimp   *noun*

Shrimps are **crustaceans**. There are over
500 species of shrimp, found in seas all
around the world. They are related to **crabs**
and **lobsters**, but shrimps are mostly small,
with a lighter, flattened body. They have five
pairs of legs for walking, and five pairs of
feathery legs for swimming. Shrimps and
prawns look very much alike but prawns are
usually larger. Shrimps have a flatter body
than a prawn and only one pair of pincers.
Many shrimps, especially in the tropics, are
camouflaged in beautiful colours, to match
their backgrounds.

skeleton ► page 136

skin   *noun*

Skin is the covering of an animal's body. It is
an **organ** that forms a protective layer over
the body. The skin of land animals stops
them drying out. It helps **warm-blooded**
animals to control their body temperature.
If an animal gets too hot, blood vessels in
the skin widen and let out heat. Skin is also
a **sense** organ, and is sensitive to touch.
Many animals which burrow or swim have a
smooth skin. Animals in cold regions have
very hairy skin to protect them from wet and
freezing weather.

skink   *noun*

Skinks are small **lizards**. There are about
900 species of skink. They are found in most
parts of the world, especially in warm
regions. Skinks live on the ground or
underground. They have a very smooth,
round body and short legs. Some skinks
have no legs at all. They have scaly skin
which may be brightly coloured. Skinks feed
on insects and small invertebrates. Some of
the largest species are **herbivorous**. Most
species of skink lay eggs, but some give
birth to live young.

skua   *noun*

Skuas are dark-coloured sea **birds**. There
are six species of skua, which are found
across all the oceans. Skuas mostly breed in
the Antarctic and Arctic regions, and around
the north Atlantic. They are powerful birds,
with a sharp, hooked bill and webbed feet,
like **gulls**. Several species have long central
tail feathers, and all have mainly brown
plumage. Skuas are **scavengers**. They
often chase other sea birds and force them
to give up the food they are carrying. Skuas
also kill other birds and mammals for
themselves.

skull   *noun*

A skull is a part of the **skeleton** of vertebrate
animals. It is the hard, bony structure which
surrounds the **brain**. The skull also protects
the **eyes**, and supports the jawbone.

skunk *noun*
Skunks are **mammals**. There are 13 species of skunk, all found in North, Central and South America. Skunks are **carnivores** and belong to the **weasel** family. They have black and white fur, short legs and a bushy tail. Skunks spray a foul-smelling liquid when disturbed or attacked. Skunks are **nocturnal**. They sleep during the day and are active at night. Skunks eat insects, small mammals, eggs and fruit.

sloth *noun*
Sloths are slow-moving **mammals**. There are five species of sloth, all found in the **rain forests** of South America and Central America. Two species have two toes, and three have three toes. Sloths are related to **armadillos** and **anteaters**. They live in the branches of trees and spend most of their time upside down. They can even sleep hanging upside down. Sloths are well **camouflaged** by their greyish fur, which is often covered with green, dust-like algae. Sloths eat mostly leaves.

slow-worm *noun*
Slow-worms are a kind of **lizard**. Unlike most lizards, slow-worms have no visible legs, so they look rather like small snakes. Slow-worms live under stones, leaves and loose soil. They like to eat small, soft-bodied animals, such as slugs. Slow-worms are sometimes called blindworms.

slug *noun*
Slugs are **molluscs**. They are related to **snails**. There are about 77,000 species in the slug and snail family. Unlike snails, most slugs have no outer hard shell. Some have a small, shield-like shell. Slugs live in damp places where they eat the leaves and stems of plants. They creep slowly along the ground, leaving behind a trail of sticky **mucus**.

snail *noun*
Snails are **molluscs**. They are related to **slugs**. There are about 77,000 species in the slug and snail family. Snails have a single, spiral shell which protects their body. When danger threatens, the snail can pull itself inside its hard shell. Most species of snail live in the sea, but some live in fresh water, and some on land. Snails creep slowly along on their flat, muscular foot.

snake *noun*
Snakes are **reptiles**. There are about 2,700 species of snake, and they are found in all countries. Snakes have a long, narrow body without any limbs. Snakes range in length from just a few centimetres to 12 metres. They move by sliding along the ground or by throwing their body into rippling loops. About 300 species of snake are **poisonous**. Most snakes eat other animals, such as small mammals and birds. Some also eat eggs.

snout ► nose

skeleton *noun*

A skeleton is the strong framework which supports the body of an animal. The skeleton of a **vertebrate** lies inside its body. This skeleton is usually made of **bone**, but it can be made of **cartilage**. The skeleton supports the body and protects soft parts inside it. The skeleton makes the body move when the **muscles** attached to the bones move. Some **invertebrate** animals have by a hard covering, called the **exoskeleton**.

At the front and the back end of the spine, there is usually a pair of limbs. Each limb is made of three areas — one long bone close to the body, then a pair of long bones and then a number of smaller bones. These smaller bones make up the feet.

pelvis

A fish has no arms or legs. The fish can move the spines that run through the fins and so control its swimming.

foot bones

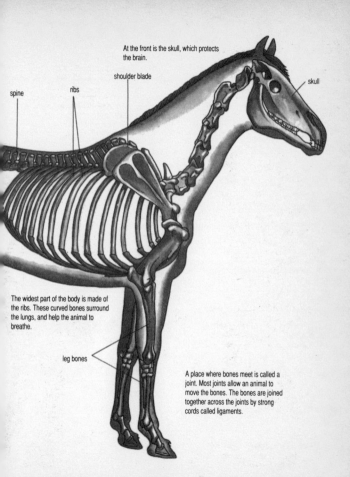

At the front is the skull, which protects the brain.

shoulder blade

spine

ribs

skull

The widest part of the body is made of the ribs. These curved bones surround the lungs, and help the animal to breathe.

leg bones

A place where bones meet is called a joint. Most joints allow an animal to move the bones. The bones are joined together across the joints by strong cords called ligaments.

social insect ► page 140

soldier ► **social insect**

spawn *verb*
Spawn describes the coming together of animals for egg-laying. Many animals, such as **frogs**, **toads** and **fish**, breed by spawning. Spawning animals often seek out a special place in water, such as a patch of ocean, or a shallow pond, before laying their eggs.

spawn *noun*
Spawn is a mass of eggs that is laid in water by some aquatic animals. **Crustaceans**, **fish** and **amphibians** all lay spawn.

species (plural **species**) *noun*
A species is a group of similar animals. Male and female animals in the same species are able to **breed** together to produce more of their own kind. Different species cannot usually breed together. The giant **panda** is one species, but the red panda is another species. They cannot reproduce young together.

sperm *noun*
Sperms are the male sex **cells**. When animals **reproduce**, the male's sperms meet **eggs** of the female. A sperm joins with an egg cell in the process of **fertilization**. A new baby animal may then develop from the fertilized egg.

spider *noun*
Spiders are **arthropods**. They belong to the group called **arachnids**, which also includes **scorpions**, **ticks** and **mites**. There are about 74,000 species of arachnid. Spiders have a rounded body, and four pairs of jointed legs. They also have strong jaws with fangs. Some spiders have a **poisonous bite**. Most spiders make a web out of silk from their own body. They trap insects, such as flies and moths, in their web, and then eat them.

spine *noun*
A spine is part of the **skeleton** of **vertebrate** animals. It is the line of small bones, called vertebrae, which surround and protect the spinal cord. The spine runs from the base of the **skull** to the hips. In animals with a tail, the spine continues to the tip of the tail. Spine is also the word used for any sharp part of an animal's body. Animals use their spines to protect them from attack. **Sea urchins** are covered with spines. Many **fish** have spines along their back.

spiny anteater *noun*
Spiny anteaters are **monotreme mammals**. There are two species of spiny anteater, which are also known as echidnas. They live in damp **forests** in parts of Australia and New Guinea. Unlike most mammals, spiny anteaters lay **eggs** and have no teeth. They have a rounded body, covered in sharp spines, and a very long, sensitive nose which they use to search for ants and worms in the soil. They lick up insects with their long, sticky tongue. Female spiny anteaters **incubate** their egg in a pouch on their abdomen.

spiny-finned fish *noun*
Spiny-finned fish are the largest group of **bony fish**. There are about 10,500 species of them. They are found throughout the world, in the sea and in fresh water. Examples of spiny-finned fish are **flatfish**, **pufferfish** and **sticklebacks**.

sponge *noun*
Sponges are soft-bodied, **invertebrate** animals. There are about 5,000 species of sponge, and most of these live in the sea. Unlike most animals, sponges live fixed in one spot. But their **larvae** swim and float in the sea. Sponges feed by filtering tiny pieces of food from the water. They have a spiky skeleton, which supports their body. Bath sponges are the dried out, soft skeletons of one kind of sponge.

springbok *noun*
The springbok, or springbuck, is a **mammal**. It is a kind of **gazelle**. Springboks live on the **savanna**, in southern Africa. When surprised they can run very fast, and jump high into the air. Springboks are **herbivores** and roam about in large herds, grazing on grasses. They have short, curved horns. Their fur is brown and white, with a dark stripe along the flank and on the face. Springboks are about 80 centimetres tall.

springtail *noun*
Springtails are small, wingless **insects**. There are about 2,000 species of springtail, most of which are less than five millimetres long. Springtails live in damp places, such as in moist soil, or under logs. They can jump by suddenly flicking their body, like uncoiling a spring. Springtails help to make the soil rich by eating dead plants.

squid *noun*
Squids are **molluscs**. They are related to **octopuses**. Squids live in the sea. They swim with their fins and use their tentacles to catch prey, such as small fish. Squids can push themselves forward quickly by forcing water out through a tube, or syphon. The largest squids grow up to 20 metres long. When attacked, squids sometimes squirt out a black, ink-like liquid into the water.

squirrel *noun*
Squirrels are **rodents**. There are more than 300 species in the squirrel family, which also includes ground squirrels and **marmots**. They are found in all parts of the world. Most squirrels live in the branches of trees, where they make a nest, called a drey. But ground squirrels are more at home on or under the ground. Flying squirrels have a special skin, or membrane, and can glide through the air. Squirrels eat fruits, nuts, bark and leaves. They often make stores of food.

starfish *noun*
Starfish are star-shaped **invertebrate** animals. They belong to the same group as **sea urchins**, **sea cucumbers** and feather-stars. There are about 6,250 species in this group. All starfish live in the sea, usually on the sea-bed, or on rocks, or corals. Some are brightly coloured. Starfish walk by moving hundreds of **tube-feet** on their underside. They eat fish, worms, and even molluscs and corals.

social insect *noun*

Social insects are **insects** which live together in a **colony** and work together for the good of the whole nest. All **ants** and **termites** and some **bees** and **wasps**, are social insects. Each insect belongs to one of three groups called castes. Bee castes are queen, worker and drone. Each caste has a different role to play in the life of the colony. The insects may **communicate** using their **antennae**, by smell or by the taste of liquids on the queen's body.

The workers take care of the colony. They make the nest bigger and repair any damage. They gather food for all the insects and they look after the eggs and young insects. The workers are infertile and can never lay eggs.

eggs

young grub

mature grub

pupa

adult bee

A honey bee goes through complete metamorphosis during its life cycle. It changes from egg to grub, from grub to pupa and from pupa to adult bee.

The queen honey bee lays all the eggs in the colony. After the queen has first mated, she builds a new nest and gives birth to the first female workers. When these workers are old enough, they look after the colony.

The drones are male bees, whose only job in the hive is to fertilize new queens.

starling *noun*
Starlings are medium-sized **birds**. There are 106 species of starling, found in Europe, Africa and Asia. The common starling has spread all over the world, and it is often found in cities. Many starlings are brightly coloured, with shiny plumage. Most have a long bill and strong legs and feet. Starlings can **mimic** the songs of other birds, and many other sounds, including the human voice. Starlings eat a wide range of food, including fruit, insects, grain and lizards.

steppe habitat *noun*
Steppe habitats are lowland areas that are covered with short grasses, and have few trees. The true steppe habitat stretches across the plains of central Asia. The North American steppe habitat is called the **prairie**. Grazing animals, such as **horses** and **rabbits**, come originally from steppe habitats.

stereoscopic vision ► **eye**

stick insect *noun*
Stick insects are large **insects**. They have a long, very thin body, which looks like a twig or a stick. Stick insects belong to the same group as leaf insects. Most stick insects live in tropical **rain forests**. During the day they hang without moving in trees and shrubs. They are so well **camouflaged** that predators cannot spot them. The largest species of stick insect grows about three centimetres long.

stickleback *noun*
Sticklebacks are small **spiny-finned fish**. There are eight species of stickleback, mostly found in fresh and brackish water. Sticklebacks have a row of sharp **spines** along their back. These help them to fight off their **predators**. The male stickleback builds an underwater nest from pieces of waterweed. He attracts a female to his nest by displaying his bright red belly. She lays eggs in the nest and the male stays on guard until the young fish hatch.

stoat *noun*
The stoat, or ermine, is a long, slender **mammal**. It is a **carnivore**, which belongs to the **weasel** family. Stoats are found in North America, Europe and Asia. They live in woodland, hedges and grassland. In northern parts, when it is cold, a stoat's fur changes from its normal brown colour to a pure white, except for the tip of the tail, which is always black. Stoats catch and eat other small mammals and birds.

stork *noun*
Storks are large water **birds**. There are 17 species of stork, found throughout the world. Storks have long legs and a long, powerful bill. Their plumage is usually black, white or grey. Storks build a large nest made of twigs. They often use the same nest year after year. Storks eat small mammals, frogs, fish and insects.

sturgeon *noun*
Sturgeons are large **fish**. There are 25 species of sturgeon. They live in large rivers and seas in the northern hemisphere. The biggest species of sturgeon grow up to six metres long. Female sturgeons lay large clumps of small, black eggs. People eat these eggs as a delicacy called caviar.

sucker *noun*
Suckers are freshwater **fish**. They belong to the **minnow** family. Suckers live in rivers and lakes in North America, China and eastern Siberia. Most suckers have thick, fleshy lips which help them to suck up small water animals and plants from the river-bed.

suckle *verb*
Suckle describes feeding a young animal with **milk**. Female **mammals** suckle their young on milk from their **mammary glands**, until they are old enough to eat solid food.

sunbird *noun*
Sunbirds are small, active **birds**. There are 116 species of sunbird. They have bright, glossy plumage and a curved bill. Sunbirds live in Africa, southern Asia and northern Australia. They feed on the nectar of tropical flowers, and on insects and spiders.

sunfish *noun*
Sunfish are **bony fish**. There are two different families of sunfish. The three species in one family are large fish with a deep, flattened body. These sunfish live in the surface waters of the world's oceans. The other family contains about 30 species, found in fresh water in North America. These sunfish have a very spiny dorsal fin.

swamp habitat *noun*
Swamp habitats are areas of wet land. In a swamp habitat, the ground and plants are always wet and spongy or they are flooded regularly. Only special plants such as bog mosses and sedges can grow well in swamp habitats. Animals that live in swamp habitats include **frogs**, and waterbirds such as **ducks** and **rails**.

swan *noun*
Swans are large water **birds**. There are seven species of swan. Swans have a long neck and large wings. All species have white plumage, except the black swan of Australia and the black-necked swan of South America. Swans are the heaviest of all flying birds. They fly in a shape called a V-formation, like **geese**. Swans eat grain and water plants, and they also feed by grazing.

swallow *noun*
Swallows are graceful **birds**. There are 74 species in the family, which includes **martins**. Swallows are found all over the world, especially in open **habitats**, such as farmland and **grassland**. Swallows have pointed wings and a forked tail. They are very agile in flight. Swallows feed mostly on insects which they catch in mid-air.

swift *noun*
Swifts are small, active **birds**. There are more than 75 species of swift. Swifts have a very streamlined body with long, narrow wings. They can fly very fast. Some species reach speeds of over 145 kilometres per hour. Swifts spend most of their time in the air. They even spend the night on the wing in good weather. Swifts eat insects which they catch in mid-air.

symbiosis noun

Symbiosis is a partnership between different species of animal, or between animals and plants. **Parasites** are a form of symbiosis, but in this relationship the **host** animal is harmed. In other forms of symbiosis, both animals benefit. By helping each other, each animal increases the chance of its own survival. Some animals allow another animal to eat the harmful parasites from its body. Soft, helpless creatures may use animals to provide protection against **predators**.

A huge grouper allows a tiny cleaner wrasse to remove the parasites inside its mouth. The grouper needs the wrasse's help to stay clean.

A hermit crab carries two huge sea anemones on top of its shell. Predators avoid the sea anemone's stinging tentacles and so the crab is protected. When the crab moves to a bigger shell, it removes the sea anemones and puts them on its new shell.

The oxpecker bird runs all over big African animals without being harmed. It pecks ticks, lice and fleas off every surface of the animal's body.

The yucca moth and the yucca plant cannot survive without each other. Only the yucca moth can take pollen from the yucca flower and fertilize other yuccas. In return, some of the yucca seeds provide food for the caterpillar of the yucca moth.

The honeyguide leads a ratel to a bees' nest. The ratel opens the nest and they both feed on the honey.

swim bladder   *noun*
The swim bladder is a part inside the body of
some **fish**. It lies near the gut, and contains
gas. Fish can rest at any depth in the water
by changing the amount of gas inside the
swim bladder.

swordfish   *noun*
The swordfish is a large sea **fish**. Its upper
jaw is long and flattened and looks like a
sword. Swordfish grow to about 4.5 metres
long. They swim very fast near the surface
of the oceans, where they catch and eat
other fish. The swordfish has a tall fin, like a
shark's, on its back.

symbiosis ► page 144

tadpole ► **frog** and **amphibian**

talon   *noun*
Talons are the feet of **birds of prey**. Talons
have long, sharp claws and powerful toes.
Birds use their talons to catch and kill prey,
such as small mammals and other birds.

tamarin   *noun*
Tamarins are small **monkeys**. There are
11 species, found in the **rain forests** of
South America. Tamarins live in groups
among the branches of trees. They have a
long, furry tail and some have long hair on
their head and round their face. They are
slightly larger than their relatives, the
marmosets. Tamarins eat mainly insects
and fruit.

tanager   *noun*
Tanagers are colourful **birds**. There are
about 200 species of tanager. They belong
to the same family as **buntings** and
honeycreepers. Tanagers are found in North
America and South America, mostly in the
tropical regions. Many tanagers are very
brightly coloured, with red, blue and yellow
plumage. They eat fruits, nectar and insects.

tapeworm   *noun*
Tapeworms are a kind of **flatworm**. They
live as **parasites** inside the gut of other
animals, mostly **vertebrates**. They attach
themselves by suckers and hooks on their
head. Tapeworms are ribbon-shaped and
they grow by forming new sections just
behind the head. Some can grow as long as
nine metres.

tapir *noun*
Tapirs are sturdy, hoofed **mammals**. There are four species of tapir. Three live in Central America and South America, and one in South-east Asia. Tapirs make up a family of their own. Their closest relatives are **horses** and **rhinoceroses**. Tapirs have short legs, a thick body and a short, flexible trunk. They live in tropical **rain forests**, where they rummage about feeding on leaves, twigs and buds, mainly at night.

tarantula *noun*
Tarantulas are large, hairy **spiders**. They live in **tropical** parts of the world. They catch other insects, and even small mammals and birds. Some tarantulas have a poisonous bite with which they paralyse their prey. Tarantulas have a group of eight eyes, and tufts of hair on their claws.

tarsier *noun*
Tarsiers are small, long-tailed **primates**. There are three species, found only in the tropical **rain forests** of Borneo, Sumatra and Sulawesi. Tarsiers have huge eyes and large ears, and they can swivel their heads almost full circle. They catch their prey of insects by watching quietly from a branch close to the forest floor, and pouncing. Tarsiers are most active at night.

teat ► **mammary gland**

teleost fish *noun*
Teleost fish are **fish** with a skeleton made of bone. There are more than 20,700 species of teleost fish, and over 95 per cent of all fish belong to this group. The other kinds of fish are **cartilaginous fish** and **jawless fish**. Teleost fish have scales and pairs of fins. Their gills are covered by flaps.

temperate *adjective*
Temperate describes a region or climate which is neither very hot nor very cold. Temperate regions lie between the tropics and the polar regions.

tentacle *noun*
Tentacles are finger-like parts of an **invertebrate's** body. **Jellyfish**, **corals** and many **worms** have tentacles. **Squids** and **octopuses** also have tentacles. Most animals use their tentacles to catch food.

termite *noun*
Termites are **insects**. There are more than 2,000 different species of termite. Termites live in **tropical** countries, throughout the world. They are **social insects**, living in large, underground **colonies**. Each termite colony may have more than a million members. Some species of termite build towering, mud mounds, up to six metres high. Termites feed on rotting wood and fungi. Some species damage buildings.

terrapin   *noun*
Terrapins are **reptiles**. They belong to the same **order** as **tortoises** and **turtles**. There are about 195 species of terrapin. They are found in most parts of the world, especially in **tropical** regions. Terrapin is the name used for the species which live in fresh water. In North America, they are known as turtles. Most terrapins have a flattened shell, and they all have webbed feet for swimming. Some have a patterned shell. Terrapins are **carnivores**, and eat other animals, such as fish, crustaceans and molluscs.

terrestrial   *adjective*
Terrestrial describes an animal or a **habitat** which is found on land. Those found in water are called **aquatic**. Terrestrial habitats include **deserts**, **forests** and **steppes**. Most **mammals** are terrestrial, but some animals, such as **amphibians**, are both terrestrial and aquatic.

thorax   *noun*
A thorax is part of the body of an **invertebrate** animal. The body of many invertebrates is divided into three parts. These are the **head**, the thorax and the **abdomen**. The thorax is the middle part, to which the animal's legs and wings are attached. The thorax itself is divided into three segments. **Insects** and **crustaceans** are the main types of invertebrate which have this kind of body with three parts.

thrush   *noun*
Thrushes are medium-sized **birds**. There are 304 species of thrush, which are found in all parts of the world. The family includes nightingales, redstarts and blackbirds. Many species of thrush are brown or grey, often with a pale, speckled or spotted breast. Some species are brightly coloured, with red, orange or blue plumage. They are strong fliers, and many species make long **migrations**. Many thrushes have attractive, musical songs. Thrushes eat insects, worms, fruits and seeds.

tick   *noun*
Ticks are tiny **arthropods** with eight legs. They are related to **spiders**, **scorpions** and **mites**. There are about 800 species of tick. They live as **parasites** on vertebrates such as reptiles, birds and mammals. Adult ticks have an oval body and eight legs which stick out on either side like a crab's legs. Ticks pierce the skin with their sharp mouthparts, and feed on blood.

tiger   *noun*
A tiger is a large, strong **mammal**. It is the biggest member of the **cat** family. Tigers live mostly in **forest** and **jungle habitats**. They are found in India, south-east China and Indonesia. A tiger has a very powerful, muscular body. Its fur has a bold pattern of black and orange stripes. Tigers are **carnivores**. They eat large mammals such as deer, which they kill using their sharp teeth. Tigers are very **rare** and may one day become **extinct** in the wild.

tinamou   *noun*
Tinamous are plump **birds**. There are 47 species of tinamou, which are found in South America and southern Mexico. Tinamous have brown or grey, streaked plumage, and a rounded body. They make whistling calls like the sound of a flute. Tinamous nest and feed on the ground, in **forests** and scrubland. They eat seeds, berries and insects. The male tinamou looks after the eggs and the young birds.

tit *noun*

Tits are small **birds**. There are 62 species of tit. They are found throughout the world, except in South America and Australia. Tits live in woodland and gardens. They are active birds and are constantly flitting around the trees, looking for food. Tits feed mainly on small insects, and sometimes eat seeds and berries. Tits often come to feed at bird tables in cold weather.

toad *noun*

Toads are **amphibians**. There are about 470 species of toad. They look like **frogs**, but have rougher, sometimes warty, skin. Many species of toad are brown in colour. Most toads lay their eggs in freshwater pools or streams. Their eggs hatch into **aquatic larvae** called tadpoles, which change, or **metamorphose**, into small, adult toads. Most adult toads spend their life on land, only returning to the water to breed.

tooth ► page 150

tortoise *noun*

Tortoises are **reptiles**. They belong to the same **order** as **terrapins** and **turtles**. Unlike turtles and terrapins, tortoises are **terrestrial** and live all their life on land. They move slowly on their leathery, clawed feet. Tortoises have no teeth, but they can bite with their hard, horny jaws. Tortoises eat plants and fruit. Some tortoises have been known to live for over a hundred years.

toucan *noun*

Toucans are **tropical birds**. There are about 40 species of toucan. They are found in the tropical **rain forests** and woods of Central America and South America. Toucans have bright plumage. It is usually black and white, with yellow or red patches. Toucans have a huge, deep bill, which they use to pluck fruit and seeds from thin twigs. They also eat reptiles, young nestling birds and eggs.

tree shrew *noun*

Tree shrews are small, **tropical mammals**. There are 18 species of tree shrew. They are found in the **forests** of India, South-east Asia and southern China. Tree shrews have a pointed nose like a **shrew**. But they otherwise look more like **squirrels**, with their long body and long, furry tail. Tree shrews only feed their babies every two days, so the babies suck a lot of milk at each feed.

treecreeper *noun*

Treecreepers are small **birds**. There are 14 species of treecreeper. They are found in all continents except South America. Treecreepers spend most of their time climbing up tree trunks and along branches, occasionally flitting from one tree to another. They search in the bark for small insects, using their thin, curved bill. Most species of treecreeper have brown or grey plumage, which acts as **camouflage** and makes them hard to spot.

trilobite *noun*
Trilobites were **arthropods**, which lived between about 300 and 600 million years ago. They are now **extinct**. About 10,000 species of trilobite have been described from **fossils**. Trilobites probably lived in shallow seas and crawled about on the mud. They ranged in length from about 2 to about 80 centimetres. Trilobites had a hard shell to protect them. They had several pairs of jointed legs and many of these legs had gills, for breathing.

tropical *adjective*
Tropical describes a living thing or a **habitat** found between the tropics of Cancer and Capricorn. In tropical areas, the Sun is often directly overhead and the temperature may rise very high. Frosts are unknown, or very rare. Tropical habitats, especially **rain forests**, have more species of animal than anywhere else on Earth.

tropicbird *noun*
Tropicbirds are graceful sea **birds**. There are three species of tropicbird. They nest in colonies on lonely **tropical** islands. But tropicbirds spend most of their life out over the open seas. They have very long, trailing feathers in the centre of their tail and brilliant white plumage. Tropicbirds feed on squid and fish, especially flying fish. They dive down into the water from the air to catch their prey.

trout *noun*
Trout are river **fish**. There are three species of true trout, which belong to the **salmon** family. They are called the brown trout, the rainbow trout and the cut-throat trout. Trout are found in rivers and seas in the northern hemisphere. They have also been introduced to freshwater habitats in **temperate** parts of the southern hemisphere. All trout have strong teeth and a streamlined body with small scales. Trout are **carnivores** and eat fish, insects and other small animals.

tuatara *noun*
A tuatara is a **reptile**. It is only found on certain islands off the north coast of New Zealand. It is very similar to **fossil** reptiles which became extinct 140 million years ago. So the tuatara is sometimes called a living fossil. Tuataras grow very slowly, and they can live to be over 100 years old.

tube-foot *noun*
Tube-feet are the feet of **starfish** and animals related to starfish. The underside of a starfish is covered with rows of these tube-shaped feet. They are joined to a system of water channels in the starfish's body. As the tube-feet move, the starfish glides slowly over the sea-bed. A starfish usually has about 1,200 tube-feet.

tuna *noun*
Tuna are large, active sea **fish**. There are 13 species of tuna, which belong to the **mackerel** family. Tuna swim fast near the surface of the sea, where they catch and eat squid and smaller fish. The largest species of tuna are four metres in length. Tuna have red, meaty flesh which is very good to eat.

tundra habitat *noun*
Tundra habitats are **habitats** which are found in and around the polar regions. They lie mainly around the North Pole, and on some high mountain ranges. Trees cannot grow in tundra habitats, and the ground is covered with mosses, sedges and shrubs. The soil is frozen and covered in snow for several months of the year. Many arctic birds, such as **ducks** and **waders**, nest in a tundra during the warmer months.

149

tooth (plural **teeth**) *noun*

A tooth is one of the very hard, bone-like parts which sit in the jaw in the mouth. There are three main types of tooth. The molars are large, flat teeth at the back of the mouth. Animals such as the **oryx** use these for chewing food. The incisors are sharp teeth at the front of the mouth. Animals such as the **beaver** use these for gnawing. The canines lie between the incisors and the molars. They are large, pointed spikes. Animals such as the **lion** use these for catching and tearing prey. Some animals also use their teeth for defence.

A lion

An oryx

A beaver

A snake has two long, sharp front teeth called fangs. Most poisonous snakes have hollow fangs. These are linked to the glands where poison is made. The snake sinks its fangs into its prey and injects the animal with venom.

The walrus has extra long canines. These show how important the walrus is. It uses them to defend itself from polar bears, to chop ice and to pull itself from the water onto the ice.

Carnivores, such as lions, have strong, sharp teeth. They use them to catch hold of their prey and to rip the flesh.

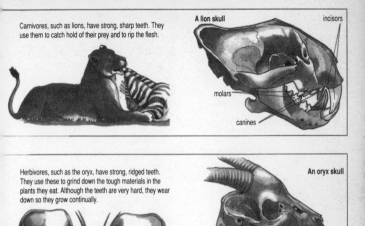

A lion skull

incisors

molars

canines

Herbivores, such as the oryx, have strong, ridged teeth. They use these to grind down the tough materials in the plants they eat. Although the teeth are very hard, they wear down so they grow continually.

An oryx skull

molars

incisors

Beavers use their strong front teeth for tearing at bark. They can chop down trees to use for building their dams. The incisors wear down, so they grow through the whole of the beaver's life.

A beaver skull

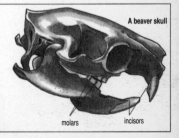

molars

incisors

turtle *noun*
Turtles are **reptiles**. They belong to the
same **order** as **tortoises** and **terrapins**.
True turtles live in the sea, and there are
seven species. Sea turtles have a large,
streamlined body. They can swim well, but
are very clumsy on land. They come up onto
a beach to lay their eggs in the sand. In
North America, the word turtle is also used
for terrapins.

tusk *noun*
Tusks are long **teeth**, sticking out from the
mouth of a **mammal**. Several kinds of
mammal have tusks, including **elephants**,
walruses, wild **pigs** and **hippopotamuses**.
Some mammals use their tusks for feeding.
Elephants use their tusks to help them push
over trees. Pigs use them for digging, or
rooting, in the ground. Other mammals use
their tusks for displaying and for fighting.

udder ► **mammary gland**

umbilical cord *noun*
An umbilical cord is a kind of tube.
It connects a mammal **embryo** to the part of
its mother called the placenta. Blood passes
through the umbilical cord between the
growing embryo and the mother. It carries
food and oxygen to the embryo. After the
baby is born, the umbilical cord dries up and
falls off. The scar it leaves behind is called
the navel.

ungulate *noun*
Ungulates are **mammals** with **hooves** on
their feet. They include even-toed ungulates,
odd-toed ungulates, elephants, hyraxes and
the aardvark. Even-toed ungulates are the
largest group. It includes pigs,
hippopotamuses, camels, deer, giraffes,
goats and antelopes. Odd-toed ungulates
include horses, zebras and rhinoceroses.

univalve *noun*
Univalves are **molluscs**. Their body is
enclosed in a single shell, unlike **bivalves**,
which have two shells. Most univalves are
gastropods, such as sea snails and land
snails.

V

vampire bat *noun*
Vampire bats are small, flying **mammals**.
There are three species, which are all found
in Central America and South America. The
most common species bites the legs of
sleeping cattle or horses and then licks up
the blood that oozes out. The other two
species feed mainly on birds' blood.

venom *noun*
Venom is poison which is made by the body
of an animal. Many animals protect
themselves by making venom. Many fish,
such as **pufferfish**, have venomous spines.
Some **toads** have venom in their skin. Many
snakes and **spiders** have a venomous bite.
venomous *adjective*

ventral ► **fin or fish**

vertebrate *adjective*
Vertebrate describes an animal which has a
spine. There are seven groups of vertebrate
animal. These are jawless fish, cartilaginous
fish, bony fish, amphibians, reptiles, birds
and mammals. There are about 40,000
species of vertebrate animal. Animals
without a spine are known as **invertebrate**
animals.

vicuña *noun*
A vicuña is a **mammal**. It is the smallest
member of the **camel** family. A vicuña lives
in the mountains of South America, at a
height of around 4,000 metres. Vicuñas
have a long, curving neck and light brown
fur, with long white hairs on the chest.
Vicuñas roam about in herds, grazing on the
rocky **grassland**.

viper *noun*
Vipers are **reptiles**. They are **venomous
snakes**, which belong to the same family as
pit vipers and **rattlesnakes**. Vipers live in
Africa, Asia, Europe and the East Indies.
The carpet or saw-scaled viper is the most
dangerous of all venomous snakes. It is
common in farming areas of Africa.

vireo *noun*
Vireos are small, woodland **birds**. There are
43 species of vireo, which are found in North
America and South America. Vireos are
mainly green, grey or brown above, with
yellow or white underparts. They live in
forests and scrubland and eat insects and
fruits. Vireos build a small nest which looks
like a bag slung from a twig of a tree.

vole noun
Voles are small **rodents**. There are
110 species of vole, which are found mainly
in North America, Europe and Asia. Voles
have a blunt nose, and small ears and eyes.
Their tail is usually about half the length of
their body. In cold weather, voles stay below
the ground in their tunnels until it becomes
warmer. Voles eat mostly grasses, roots and
berries.

vulture *noun*
Vultures are large **birds of prey**. There are
22 species of vulture in two groups. New
World vultures are found in North America
and South America. Old World vultures live
in Europe, Africa and Asia. The Andean
condor is a species of New World vulture. It
is the largest of all birds of prey, with a
wingspan of nearly three metres. Vultures
have broad wings and a long neck. They
have bare patches on their face and neck.
Vultures feed mainly on **carrion**.

W

wader *noun*
Waders are active shore **birds**. There are
about 200 species of wader, which are found
in all parts of the world. **Plovers**, snipes and
sandpipers are all types of wader. Waders
have long, thin legs. They feed along the
sea-shore, or on mudbanks of rivers and
lakes. Waders eat small water animals
hidden in the sand or mud. Some waders
have a long bill to help them reach their
prey. **Avocets** have an upturned bill which
they sweep sideways through the water.

wallaby *noun*
Wallabies are **marsupial mammals**. They
belong to the largest of the **kangaroo**
families, which contains about 50 species.
They are found in Australia and New
Guinea. The smaller species are usually
called wallabies, and the larger ones
kangaroos. Wallabies have strong back legs
and move along by jumping. Females have
a **pouch**. Most wallabies live in **grassland
habitats**, where they graze. Some live on
rocky hills, and others in **forest habitats**.

walrus *noun*
A walrus is a large sea **mammal**. Walruses
live in the Arctic seas and are related to
seals and **sea-lions**. They have a large, fat
body. Both male and female walruses have
a pair of long tusks, pointing downwards
from their mouth. Walruses use their tusks
for grubbing in the sea-bed and to help lever
themselves out of the water. Adult male
walruses can reach a length of over three
metres. A walrus's favourite food is
molluscs.

warbler *noun*
Warblers are small **birds**. There are about 570 species in three main families. Old World warblers are found mainly in Europe and Asia. Australian warblers live in and around Australia. Wood warblers live in North America and South America. Old World and Australian warblers are mostly dull-coloured. Many wood warblers have bright, colourful plumage. All warblers are **insectivores**. Many have musical songs.

warm-blooded *adjective*
Warm-blooded describes an animal which can control its own body temperature. The opposite of warm-blooded is **cold-blooded**. **Birds** and **mammals** are warm-blooded, but all other animals are cold-blooded.

warren *noun*
Warrens are the groups of **burrows** which some **rabbits** make underground. In a warren, there is a complicated system of tunnels, and many families of rabbits live close together. Baby rabbits are born in special parts of the warren, which the females line with plant material and fur.

wart hog *noun*
A wart hog is a **mammal**. It is a large species of **pig**. Wart hogs live in **savanna** and **forest habitats** of Africa. They have a long face, with several wart-like knobs of skin and two pairs of curved tusks. Wart hogs use their tusks for fighting. They feed mostly on grasses, grass seeds and roots.

wasp *noun*
Wasps are **insects**. There are about 17,000 species of wasp, found all over the world. Many wasps have a striped abdomen, usually brightly coloured in yellow or orange and black. Wasps fly well, using two pairs of transparent wings. Many wasps are **social insects**, and live in large **colonies**. They eat other insects, and also fruit and nectar. Wasps have a powerful sting, which they use in defence or to catch their prey.

water buffalo *noun*
The water buffalo is a large, strong **mammal**. It is related to cows, and has heavy, curved horns. It is found wild in India, Nepal, Assam and Burma. Tamed, or **domesticated**, water buffaloes have spread to other countries, such as North Africa, southern Europe, South America and Australia. Water buffaloes spend a lot of their time wallowing in water and wet mud. This helps them keep cool in hot climates. Water buffaloes eat grass and other plants.

waterbuck *noun*
The waterbuck is a **mammal**. It belongs to the antelope family. Waterbuck live in Africa, in **forest** and **savanna habitats**, close to rivers or lakes. They have shaggy, waterproof fur. Male waterbuck have long horns, which are slightly curved forwards. Waterbuck graze on grasses, reeds, rushes and water plants. They often stand knee-deep in the water when feeding.

155

wing *noun*

A wing is the part of the body which some animals use to fly. Animals have pairs of wings. All **birds** have one pair of wings, even though a few birds do not fly. The wings are covered in **feathers** which help the bird control its flight. Most **insects** have two pairs of wings, though they may only use one pair for flight.

A bird's wing is made of muscle and feathers. It is supported at the front by the bones of the bird's front limb.

The wandering albatross has the longest wings. The wing span, the distance from wing tip to wing tip, is more than three metres.

Penguins use their wings for swimming. Their feathers are short and stumpy.

A bat's wings are made of a thin membrane spread between its long fingers. If a bat damages the membrane, the wing will not heal and the bat cannot fly.

The flying phalanger does not really have wings. It has thin flaps of skin between its legs. It uses these like a tiny parachute when it glides from tree to tree.

Insect wings

Honey bees use both wings to fly. They beat their wings 225 times a second.

Beetles use only their delicate back wings to fly and beat them 50 times a second.

Butterflies flap both wings at the same time eight to 12 times a second.

Flies only have front wings which they beat 200 times a second.

weasel *noun*
Weasels are small, slender **mammals**.
There are 12 species of weasel, which are
found in North America, South America,
Europe, Africa and Asia. Weasels are expert
hunters, especially underground, or beneath
snow. They can easily follow tunnels with
their slim, bendy bodies. They eat small
mammals such as voles, mice, and even
larger species such as rats and rabbits. The
common weasel is smaller than the stoat,
and lacks the black tail tip.

weaver *noun*
Weavers are small, perching **birds**. There
are 143 species in the weaver family, which
also includes **sparrows**. True weavers are
found mainly in Africa. A few species live in
Asia. Most female weavers are plain-
coloured. But the males of most species
have bright red or yellow plumage in the
mating season. Weavers are noisy birds and
many species nest in **colonies**. They weave
their nest from twigs and grass stems, hung
in a tree.

web *noun*
A web is a trap made of silk by a **spider**.
Spiders produce silk threads from their own
body, and use these to build a web. The silk
of the web is very thin, but also very strong.
Some threads are sticky. When a flying
insect crashes into a spider's web, it may
get stuck. The spider then rushes out and
paralyses the insect with a **bite**, before
wrapping it up in a silk bundle.

webbed foot ► **foot**

weevil *noun*
Weevils are **beetles**. There are more than
50,000 species in the weevil family, which
also includes bark beetles. Adult weevils
have a long, pointed snout, with jointed
feelers sticking out on either side. Some
species of weevil, such as the rice weevil
and the cotton-boll weevil, are serious **pests**
that attack crops.

whale *noun*
Whales are large **marine mammals**. There
are about 75 species in two main groups.
The toothed whales include **killer whales**,
pilot whales, **porpoises** and **dolphins**. They
feed on squid and fish. Killer whales also eat
seals and birds. The baleen whales include
the blue whale and the humpback whale.
They feed by filtering **zooplankton** from the
water. The blue whale is the largest mammal
ever to have lived on Earth. It can reach a
length of about 27 metres.

wild horse *noun*
A wild horse is a large **mammal**. It is the
ancestor of all **domesticated** horses. The
wild horse lives in open plains in Mongolia,
and is also called Przewalski's horse. It is
very **rare** in the wild, but there are a few
herds in zoos and game parks. In many
other places there are also wild horses. But
these are descended from domestic horses
which have become **feral**.

wildebeest ► **gnu**

wing ► page 156

wolf *noun*
Wolves are dog-like **mammals**. The two
species of wolf belong to the **dog** family. The
grey wolf is found in northern parts of North
America and in Asia and Europe. The red
wolf is now probably **extinct** in the wild.
Wolves live in family groups, or packs, of up
to about 20 members. They eat a wide
range of smaller mammals.

wolverine *noun*
A wolverine is a sturdy, medium-sized **mammal**. It belongs to the **weasel** family. Wolverines are found in the northern parts of North America, Europe and Asia, and in the Arctic region. They have large feet with strong claws and they can move quickly over snow. Wolverines eat mammals, birds and carrion. They are very strong for their size, and can kill animals as large as reindeer. Wolverines store uneaten food and return to it later when they are hungry. The wolverine is **rare** today because it was hunted in the past for its fur.

wombat *noun*
Wombats are **marsupial mammals**. There are three main species of wombat, which are found in southern and eastern Australia. Wombats have short legs, a large head, and a thick, heavy body. They are active at night, and live in **burrows** which they dig in the soil. Wombats eat grass and roots which they chew with their strong teeth.

woodland ► forest

woodlouse *noun*
Woodlice are land **crustaceans**. They are found all over the world. Woodlice live mainly in damp **habitats**, such as beneath logs and stones. They have seven pairs of legs. Woodlice eat decaying leaves, vegetables and fruit. Woodlice can roll their body up into a tight ball when they are threatened.

woodpecker *noun*
Woodpeckers are small or medium-sized **birds**. There are about 200 species, which are found all over the world. Woodpeckers have special feet with two toes pointing forwards, and two pointing backwards. This helps them to climb on tree trunks. Woodpeckers have a long, sharp bill which they use to dig holes in tree trunks and branches. They do this to find insects under the bark, or to make a nest hole.

worker ► social insect

worm *noun*
Worms are tube-shaped **invertebrate** animals. They are divided into three main groups. There are about 25,000 species of **flatworm**, which have a ribbon-shaped body. Flatworms include **flukes** and **tapeworms**. There are about 15,000 species of **roundworm**. They have a rounded body, without rings or segments. Examples of roundworms are **hookworms** and eelworms. There are about 15,000 species of segmented worm, including **earthworms**, **leeches** and bristleworms.

wren *noun*
Wrens are small perching **birds**. There are about 63 species of wren, found in North America, Europe and Asia. Wrens have a plump body, short wings and a thin, sharp bill. They move quickly through the undergrowth, and pick small insects off plants. Most wrens have brown or grey plumage. Some species have loud, musical songs.

Y

Z

yak *noun*
A yak is a large **mammal**. It is a member of the same family as antelope, goats, bison and gnus. It lives high in the mountains and plateaux of Tibet. Yaks have a heavy body and very thick, shaggy fur. Their fur keeps them warm in their very cold **habitat**. Yaks are sometimes tamed, or **domesticated**, and used as farm animals.

yolk *noun*
Yolk is part of an **egg** of a **vertebrate** animal. **Reptiles**, and especially **birds**, lay eggs with a large yolk. It acts as a store of food for the growing **embryo**. The yolk in a bird's egg is yellow in colour. As the baby bird develops, it gradually uses up all the food in the yolk.

young *adjective*
Young describes animals which are not fully grown, or adult. In some animals, such as most **invertebrates**, the young look quite different from the adults. These animals go through a process of **metamorphosis** from the young stage to the adult stage. The young of some **vertebrate** animals, such as **amphibians**, are also quite different from the adults. But in most vertebrates, the young look like small adults.

zebra *noun*
Zebras are large, striped **mammals**. There are three species of zebra, which are related to **horses**. They are all found in eastern and southern Africa. Zebras have the build of a pony, but their coat has a bold pattern of black and white stripes. They also have a stiff mane along their neck. Zebras live in herds on the open **plain** and **savanna**, where they graze on grasses.

zoologist *noun*
A zoologist is someone who studies **zoology**.

zoology *noun*
Zoology is the study of animals. It deals with the naming and grouping, or **classification**, of wild species. It looks at how animals' bodies work, and studies their **behaviour**. It may look at the genetics of animals, or how **characteristics** pass from one generation to the next.
zoological *adjective*

zooplankton *noun*
Zooplankton is the name used for the tiny animals which float or swim in the sea. It is carried along by ocean currents. Zooplankton forms part of **plankton**. It is made up of many different kinds of animal. It includes the **larvae** of molluscs, jellyfish, crustaceans, starfish, worms and fish.